ORSON'S SHADOW
SHADOW

BY AUSTIN PENDLETON

**WITH AN INTRODUCTION
BY ROBERT SIMONSON**

★

★

DRAMATISTS
PLAY SERVICE
INC.

2

for David Cromer

INTRODUCTION

"Don't plead, Orson. It frightens me to hear you plead. Don't plead. Ever again."

This line — said by Laurence Olivier after he has gently and suddenly fired his director, Orson Welles — is the last one naturalistically spoken by any character in Austin Pendleton's bristling, bracing play *Orson's Shadow*. In it, one can read in miniature the whole of Pendleton's searching, painfully hilarious and endlessly compassionate examination of his own tortured profession.

Olivier, in the playwright's conceit, is being directed by Welles in the 1960 London premiere of Eugene Ionesco's *Rhinocernos* (an actual event, though as a human interaction here almost wholly imagined by Pendleton). By telling Welles not to plead, Olivier is not scolding his colleague. He is speaking plainly; he is frightened, even terrified. Orson Welles, perhaps the greatest would-have-been in artistic history, "fails," as Olivier bluntly puts it earlier in the play. Olivier generally succeeds. "He always has a triumph. It is his strategy for absolutely everything," says Welles. But in Orson, the man who was postwar England's finest actor sees (indeed, everyone in the play sees) the potentially yawning chasm of failure.

At first Laurence arms himself against this Wellesian ebb tide. Finally, in a desperate bid for personal and professional preservation, he flees from it, as well as from the different sort of failure (not of the self-sabotaging hubris variety but of crippling self-doubt) represented by his first wife, mentally unstable actress Vivien Leigh. He runs in the direction of the second Mrs. Olivier, Joan Plowright, who shares with Olivier the ability to keep her head while all those about her are losing theirs. He takes more hesitant steps in the direction of famed critic Kenneth Tynan, who knows how to hold his own among these giants, while nonetheless courting physical disaster through chain-smoking.

Olivier's succinct utterance is only one line in Pendleton's lingually zingy script that could be taken as a perfect epigram for the creative life, passages that seem to have been plucked from *Bartlett's*. Others include:

"One shows brilliant early promise and then one travels."

"What I see now is that they've [artists] done anything of any worth at all is a miraculous achievement. Because they are in fact insane."

"He's a living genius, and once one is called a living genius one only exists to disappoint."

I doubt that someone who knew only playwriting could have created this play, so empathetic of every corner of the theatre. But Pendleton is not solely a playwright, and thus is singularly equipped to understand these fatalistic sentiments and the plights of those who embody them. He has been nearly everything in his four-decades-plus career. Like Welles, Olivier, Plowright and Leigh, he is an actor (once sharing a screen with Orson). Like Welles and Olivier, he also knows the directing trade. He has run a theatre company, as Olivier did, and, of course, shares with Welles a talent for the written word. He has never been a drama critic — Tynan's chief claim to fame — but is unique among his associates in having shown a certain comprehension of and respect for that necessary profession. Above all, he knows well the ups and downs, fears and desires of which all the major characters in *Orson's Shadow* are acutely aware.

Pendleton brings another rare talent to the subjects in question. As he illustrated in his earlier play, *Booth*, he understands how the famous, immortal and iconic should speak — at least onstage. The challenge of finding the right dialogue to stuff into the unknowable heads and mouths of mythic figures such as Welles and Olivier would stymie many another writer. Mundanities don't sound right. Grandiloquence comes off as unreal and impersonal. Pendleton finds an everyday theatrical language that lies somewhere in the middle. Take, for instance, this section about "The War of the Worlds" broadcast spoken by Leigh to Welles:

"People fled their homes, Orson, people killed themselves, because you made them believe in all your Martians. And Larry was so jealous, and then I got the role of Scarlet O'Hara in Gone with the Wind *and he was devastated.*

And he took it out on your show about the Martians, and I said, 'Larry, oh my darling boy, you have moved people,' and he turned on me and he said, 'No one has taken to the roads. No one has actually committed suicide.' Larry sets very high standards for himself!"

Did Vivien Leigh talk like that? Who knows? But it sounds something like what she might have talked like — hectic, flighty, actressy, charming. It is a dramatic notion of how a dramatic person in a dramatic profession might conduct normal conversation.

Similarly, *Orson's Shadow* is a condensed, concentrated conjecture about how show people — grand, neurotic, needy, talented at reproductions of living but challenged by life — muddle through each day, alternately avoiding and succumbing to the despair that lurks at the lip of the stage, all for the sake of the off-chance that they might briefly achieve joyous artistic triumph. It is the best play about the dark midnight of the artistic soul in a generation. Anyone inside or outside the theatre who has casually or earnestly wondered why the names listed in any given program put themselves through hell for a few magic hours in the dark can find a few dozen answers (there has never been one single answer) in this delightful and discerning text.

—Robert Simonson
New York City
August 2005

AUTHOR'S NOTE

In the spring of 1996 my friend Judith Auberjonois invited me to her house for breakfast and to tell me of an idea she'd had. She told me that in 1960, in London, Orson Welles had directed Laurence Olivier and that by the time the play opened Orson no longer felt welcome in the project. She asked me if I'd like to write a play about it. Judith, a fine actress, has a fine, fierce visionary spirit about the theatre, and I was daunted by the idea at first, for quite a while in fact, but it was clearly a brilliant idea, and it drew me on. There was no contract, there was only faith on Judith's part, and the generosity of the idea, and it has changed my life. I thank her.

I also thank everybody who's worked on productions of this play. It was first produced in 2000, and there were several other productions after that before the New York production, as well as several lovingly rehearsed readings of it by fine theatres like New Rep in Boston and the Philadelphia Theatre Company. I have never seen a performance in this play, not a piece of direction or design, that was not excellent or more. This has helped the process of continual revision immeasurably. What has also helped it is the fact that at Steppenwolf, where the play was first produced, the dramaturg and literary manager was Michele Volansky. She is wonderful at this work. Again, my thanks to everybody.

—*Austin Pendleton*

ORSON'S SHADOW, in an earlier version, received its world premiere at the Steppenwolf Theatre (Martha Lavey, Artistic Director; Michele Volansky, Dramaturg and Literary Manager) in Chicago, Illinois, on January 16, 2000. It was directed by David Cromer; the set design was by Mark Lohman; the costume design was by Jennifer Keller; the lighting design was by J.R. Lederle; the sound design was by Chris J. Johnson; and the stage manager was James Wood. The cast was as follows, in order of appearance:

KEN .... David Warren
SEAN .... Dominic Conti
ORSON .... Jeff Still
LARRY .... John Judd
JOAN .... Sarah Wellington
VIVIEN .... Lee Roy Rogers

Subsequent productions were mounted at the Williamstown Theatre Festival (Michael Ritchie, Producing Director); the Westport Playhouse (Joanne Woodward, Artistic Director); the Old Globe Theatre (Jack O'Brien, Artistic Director); The Black Dahlia Theatre (Matt Shakman and Steven Klein, Producing Directors); and the Chicago Center of the Performing Arts (Anthony Tomaska, Producing Director). The play was directed at these theatres by David Cromer (Williamstown, Westport and CCPA), Kyle Donnelly (Old Globe) and Matt Shakman (Black Dahlia).

ORSON'S SHADOW received its New York City premiere at the Barrow Street Theatre on March 13, 2005. It was produced by Planetearth Partners (Chip Meyrelles and Tom Wirtshafter) and Scott Morfee. It was directed by David Cromer; the set design was by Takeshi Kata; the costume design was by Theresa Squire; the lighting design was by Tyler Micoleau; the sound design was by Jonah Lawrence; the property design was by Michele Spadaro; the general manager was Cris Buchner; and the production stage manager was Richard A. Hodge. The cast was as follows.

JOAN .... Susan Bennett
LARRY .... John Judd
KEN .... Tracy Letts
VIVIEN .... Lee Roy Rogers
ORSON .... Jeff Still
SEAN .... Ian Westerfer

CHARACTERS

KEN

SEAN

ORSON

LARRY

JOAN

VIVIEN

PLACE

The stage of the Gaiety Theatre in Dublin;
later, the stage of the Royal Court Theatre in London.

TIME

1960.

ORSON'S SHADOW

ACT ONE

The stage of the Gaiety Theatre in Dublin. There is a ghost light (this will change). Furniture of a medieval tavern is scattered across the stage. Kenneth Tynan enters. After a moment:

KEN. Hello? *(Silence. He turns to us.)* Where is he? *(Pause. He calls, quietly:)* Orson? *(Sean enters.)*
SEAN. *(Irish.)* Are you Ken?
KEN. Yes. Yes, I am, I —
SEAN. Orson says he'll be out soon.
KEN. Oh. M-m-m-might I go on back?
SEAN. No.
KEN. Ah. It's just that I — I usually do —
SEAN. But he says not to, Ken. He says you mustn't go.
KEN. Ah. Of course, then. *(Pause.)* Is he all right?
SEAN. Oh, yes, Ken.
KEN. Good. Good. *(Pause.)* He's not angry with me, of course.
SEAN. I don't know.
KEN. I really must go back. *(Coughs.)*
SEAN. Are you all right, Ken?
KEN. Yes, yes. It's just, it's — it's damp out there —
SEAN. Well, that's it, then.
KEN. That's what?
SEAN. That's why he's angry at you.
KEN. What have I done?
SEAN. You sent a note before the show, you said you'd be back after the show. But you didn't come, so that means you really didn't like the show.
KEN. Forgive me, but it's not that simple —
ORSON. *(Off.)* Yes, it is.

11

KEN. Orson? *(Coughs.)*

ORSON. *(Off.)* I don't like that cough, Ken. Sean, get him my robe, and some brandy and hot water.

KEN. *(As Sean goes off.)* He needn't —

ORSON. *(Off.)* I'm very upset with you, Ken. You're frail and you stand in the damp air because you're afraid to tell me you didn't like the show.

KEN. I wanted to be clear, that's all. I mean, what am I to you without my clarity?

ORSON. *(Off.)* You're my friend! That's what you are without your clarity! —

KEN. Orson, I thought you might need time to get out of all that padding! *(Silence.)* Orson?

SEAN. *(Back, with robe, brandy.)* Oh, Ken.

KEN. What have I said?

SEAN. See, Ken, he wears no padding.

KEN. Oh, Christ! I really must go back.

SEAN. No.

KEN. This is insane!

SEAN. He's afraid you're going to talk to him about that Laurence Olivier.

KEN. Look, I am trying to help him! —

ORSON. *(Off.)* Olivier destroyed me in Hollywood, did you know that?

KEN. What are you talking about?

ORSON. *(Off.)* Never mind, I'm not going into the details, but he destroyed me in Hollywood in 1948.

KEN. I am exhausted from my flight! —

ORSON. *(Off.)* I can't help that.

KEN. And I came all the way from New York!

ORSON. *(Off.)* New York? What were you doing in New York?

KEN. I've been in New York for two years, reviewing for the *New Yorker*, as I have told you many times —

ORSON. *(Off.)* Drink the brandy, Ken. I have warned you about this traveling you do, I have told you you'll get sick —

KEN. Well, Orson, you know how it is. One shows brilliant early promise and then one travels! *(Silence.)* Orson? *(Silence.)* I shouldn't have said that.

SEAN. Oh, Ken.

KEN. What?

SEAN. I feel bad for you.

KEN. It'll be all right. He's on edge. I don't blame him, stuck in Dublin of all places —

SEAN. How dare you say that to me, Ken.

KEN. I'm sorry. I am truly sorry.

SEAN. Did Orson fuck Rita Hayworth?

KEN. I beg your pardon?

SEAN. I heard he fucked Rita Hayworth.

KEN. Well, he was married to her.

SEAN. Oh.

KEN. He fucked Judy Garland.

SEAN. Oh! Who else, then.

KEN. Well — I'm sorry, what's your name?

SEAN. Sean.

KEN. Sean, might I? — *(He indicates us, moves forward and addresses us.)* I didn't want to turn that nice young man into a receptacle for exposition. However willing he might be. I mean, this could have turned into one of those dreadful scenes in which he asks me questions and I answer them, until, with clumsy spontaneity, we have told the audience the entire forty-five years of Orson's life to date. Like the maid who answers the telephone at the beginning of the play. *(He mimes a phone and imitates a maid.)* "Hello? Oh, I'm sorry, Mr. Welles has stepped out — well, you see, he's walking on the moors — well, I don't know how long, you see he's brooding — Why is he brooding? — Because they tore up 'is contract at RKO in 1941 — How many years ago was that? — Well, nineteen years, wasn't it, because you know what year it is now — You don't? — It's 1960! — Oh, it's been nineteen long and bitter years 'ere, yes, they tore up that contract after 'e made *Citizen Kane*, took away 'is right to final cut they did, and 'im having lost his mum to the jaundice when he was nine, poor little tyke — what's final cut? — well, Mr. Zanuck, final cut is where nobody can touch the filum after Mr. Welles cuts it the way 'e likes it, and they took it away after *Citizen Kane*, they did — What's *Citizen Kane*? — why, just today the gardener says to me, 'Bessie, it revolutionized the art of the motion picture! I particularly admire his use of deep focus.'" *(Back to his own voice.)* Well, you see what I mean. The plays were like that. Oh, I fought it. With every breath in my body, which is not saying a great deal because I really do smoke too much, but of course no one took really seriously a word I wrote. You see, I am a critic. What is a critic? A critic is no one. A critic is a man who cowers in a train compartment before a woman whose baleful eyes are saying, "I'm sure I have no idea why you were so unkind to poor Vivien Leigh." I tell you, I came to cherish the idea that there was more to life than this. And so I decided to approach Sir Laurence Olivier — my hero, really, in case you're interested — to ask if I might work with him to create the National Theatre of Great Britain which he is soon to form, to, well, advise him. I realized that if I'm to get him to hire me I must present him with an idea that will appall him so much he will always remember it was not his. Well, he needs a director for a play he's doing, and I'm proposing Orson. I'm using Orson. I'm using my best friend. I'm using the man I wish had been my father. My real father was not, you see, married to my mother. I am illegitimate. This is an advantage for a critic, actually, as when you write harshly of someone and they call you a bastard, you can receive it as a simple statement of fact. What is the point of what I'm saying? Oh, yes. No, I'm not using Orson, I am trying to help him. All those films he made since *Citizen Kane*, since they took away his right to final cut, all those marvelous films butchered by the studios, I feel grief, raw grief when I think about it, mitigated only slightly by the fact that it was his own fucking fault. Or much of it. Or not much of it at all, really. I don't know. Do you have friends like this? Never mind.

ORSON. Ken?

KEN. Oh! *(Ken starts to cough, in surprise. Orson has entered during the last moments of Ken's speech to us. Now he hurries to Ken.)*

ORSON. Are you all right?

KEN. Yes, I'm —

ORSON. I'll get you some more brandy and —

KEN. Don't go to your dressing room again.

ORSON. You can follow me.

KEN. No, I can't. Sean will leap out and strike me.

ORSON. I sent Sean for my food.

KEN. Your food? At this hour?

ORSON. Yes, my food, at this hour, and WHERE IS IT? Sean, where have you been?

SEAN. *(Enters.)* Getting your food.

ORSON. Thank you, Sean. Thank you. Could you turn on the lights, please?

SEAN. *(Arranging the table.)* No.

ORSON. You realize I was directing when I was younger than you are now, that I would send for the best steaks in New York at three in the morning because the actors could take naps, those bastards, but not me, and now you're asking me to eat this mutton in a ghost light?

SEAN. Yes.

ORSON. You're implying that because of a slight dip at the box office they don't have the money to turn on the lights, but, you see, they owe me, Sean. You know that, don't you.

SEAN. No.

ORSON. They owe me. And do you know why? Because of all the theatres in the world I chose theirs for this production. And Sean seems insufficiently impressed.

KEN. I told him you were married to Rita Hayworth.

ORSON. I saw Rita in the airport in Los Angeles two months ago, and she did not know who I was.

KEN. Oh, no.

ORSON. I loved that woman.

KEN. My mother died insane, of course.

ORSON. Of course I loved Hollywood, and Hollywood has not known who I am since 1948.

KEN. Now, that's not true!

ORSON. All right, it's not true. Relax.

SEAN. Could I meet Rita, Orson.

ORSON. *(Sits to eat.)* She doesn't know me, Sean. Nobody knows me. Pay attention.

KEN. He's just made his comeback film in Hollywood, so disregard —

ORSON. Have you heard what's happened?

KEN. Oh, Christ, have you botched this one?

ORSON. All I did was —

KEN. Did you walk out on this one, too?

ORSON. All I did was make such a great picture that Universal's offering me a five-picture deal.

KEN. What? That's —

ORSON. What? What is that, Ken?

KEN. That's wonderful.

ORSON. You hear that, Sean? Ken Tynan has just conceded that I have not destroyed my life in art, go get another bottle of the red.

SEAN. What's Universal, Orson.

ORSON. A big Hollywood studio.

SEAN. What pictures did they make?

ORSON. *Abbott and Costello Meet the Invisible Man.*

SEAN. Can I meet Abbott and Costello, then.

ORSON. If you turn on the lights. *(Silence.)* Come on, Sean. Sell out. *(Sean exits.)* Would you like some steak? You don't look well, I'm worried about you.

KEN. I wouldn't dream of depriving you of your two steaks.

ORSON. Look, I'm trying, I'm taking diet pills —

KEN. Well, give me the name of your doctor, then, as I must put on weight!

ORSON. Ken?

KEN. What?

ORSON. You're being a cunt. *(Stage lights come flooding on.)* Thank you, Sean! Here. *(Starts to cut food.)* Why did you hate the show?

KEN. I did not hate the show.

ORSON. *(Cutting the food.)* Well, yes, you did …

KEN. Do you really want to know what I thought?

ORSON. Salt?

KEN. It made me concerned about your state of mind.

ORSON. Oh boy.

KEN. I mean, what did you call this thing? I can't —

ORSON. *Chimes at Midnight.*

KEN. The title alone gives one a chill.

ORSON. Everything gives you a chill, Ken, it's because you're thin. Here. *(Food.)*

KEN. Shakespeare called these plays *King Henry the Fourth, Parts One and Two*!

ORSON. But these plays are about Falstaff.

KEN. Your part.

ORSON. Give me the review.

KEN. The review?

ORSON. That you were writing in the damp, which will destroy the show so I can't take it into London and get a movie made of it.

KEN. I did not come here to betray you!

ORSON. It's all right. I have a theory about Judas and it's sympathetic.

KEN. Christ! —

ORSON. Ken, I have been working on this show since I was at the Todd School for Boys. Even then, Ken, even then I wanted nothing more than to become a fat old man, this is the realization of a lifelong dream, and I'm sorry you hated it so much.

KEN. Oh, Orson, it was fucking brilliant! All right? —

ORSON. It's all right, you're jet-lagged, I understand.

KEN. It's just that the *King Henry* plays are the most exhilarating

Shakespeare ever wrote! —

ORSON. Oh, come on, Ken!

KEN. And to see you reduce them to this chilling sadness —

ORSON. Ken, you have a brilliant mind but it contains no actual information. In this play Falstaff befriends the Prince, and then, when he's to be crowned king I show up at his coronation and he pretends he does not know me, and you call this exhilarating? This is tragic! Of course you lack all tragic sense.

KEN. I do not lack all tragic sense.

ORSON. Any one who expects me to work with Larry Olivier lacks all tragic sense, because Larry Olivier —

ORSON.	KEN.
Destroyed me.	Destroyed you —

KEN. In Hollywood in 1948, I know.

ORSON. You wouldn't understand.

KEN. Of course I wouldn't understand. It isn't true.

ORSON. Are you calling me a liar?

KEN. Yes.

ORSON. Of course you are. You're a critic. You eat my food and then you call me a liar.

KEN. I don't want your food! —

ORSON. I'm worried about your health, Ken! Sean!

KEN. The person who destroyed you in Hollywood in 1948 was you yourself!

ORSON. Ken, that's a cliché. *(Calls off.)* Sean! Kenneth Tynan is talking in clichés!

KEN. You could have had anything you wanted after *Citizen Kane* —

ORSON. This is the Classic Comics version of my life! Ken!

KEN. Orson! Have you or have you not walked out on the editing of two films since Kane?

ORSON. I did not walk out on the editing of *Ambersons*!

KEN. You went to Brazil, which I know to you is a walk around the block!

ORSON. *(Overlap.)* My president ordered me to Brazil to make a documentary about —

KEN and ORSON. Inter-American relations —

ORSON. There was a war on, if you'll —

KEN. I know there was a war on! I was in England!

ORSON. Did they drop bombs on Oxford? They did not bomb Oxford. Hitler wanted very much to teach at Oxford, that is why

17

the war was fought! Sean!

SEAN. *(Appears.)* Orson.

ORSON. Had you ever heard of Laurence Olivier before Ken brought him up?

KEN. Orson!

ORSON. Had you heard of him?

SEAN. No.

ORSON. Well, now, you see, that's very moving to me, Sean.

KEN. I don't see what this —

SEAN. Who is he?

ORSON. He is the greatest actor in the English-speaking world, according to Ken.

KEN. Not just to me! —

ORSON. All right! And others.

SEAN. Is he in the movies?

ORSON. Did you see the movie of *King Henry the Fifth*?

SEAN. Yes.

ORSON. He was King Henry the Fifth.

SEAN. Oh, I like him.

ORSON. You like him?

SEAN. Yes.

ORSON. Do you know who King Henry the Fifth is?

SEAN. King of England.

ORSON. Do you know who he was before he was the King?

SEAN. The Prince.

ORSON. Prince Hal is who he was.

SEAN. Prince Hal in this play we're doing here?

ORSON. Prince Hal, who refuses to recognize me at his coronation.

SEAN. Well, you know, Orson —

ORSON. What do you mean, "well, you know, Orson" —

SEAN. I mean, you know what I think.

ORSON. No, I don't know what you think.

SEAN. Well, I think it's your fault.

ORSON. What's my fault?

SEAN. When he says what he says to you at the coronation.

ORSON. When he says, "I know thee not, old man. Fall to thy prayers."

SEAN. Yes.

ORSON. That's my fault.

SEAN. Yes.

ORSON. What do you mean, Sean? I'm his best friend, I don't

know what you mean.

SEAN. Well, you know —

ORSON. I take him drinking, I take him whoring, I take him on adventures.

SEAN. But, Orson, you know what he says at the beginning? When you're with the whores, and then you leave the stage? You know what he says.

ORSON. What.

SEAN. He turns to the audience and he says, "This isn't really me, you know, and when I'm King I'm going to change me ways and forget this fecking Falstaff."

ORSON. He says that?

SEAN. As soon as you leave the stage.

ORSON. That bastard.

SEAN. Then you come back and you keep thinking he's your friend and you go to his coronation and he don't know you, well, what do you expect. It's your fault, you know.

ORSON. He's leaving his wife.

SEAN. Who?

ORSON. Olivier. Pay attention. Olivier is leaving his wife. Vivien Leigh. Do you know her?

SEAN. No.

ORSON. *Gone with the Wind*, did you see that?

SEAN. Is she Scarlett O'Hara.

ORSON. Yes.

SEAN. Oh, I like her.

ORSON. Well, he's leaving her.

SEAN. I like that *Gone with the Wind*.

ORSON. Well, you like *Henry the Fifth*.

SEAN. Oh, yes.

ORSON. Do you like *Citizen Kane*?

SEAN. What?

ORSON. *Citizen Kane*.

SEAN. What's —

ORSON. Never mind.

SEAN. Is that a movie?

ORSON. Never mind, Sean, it's all right.

SEAN. Oh, I'm sorry, were you in that movie, Orson?

ORSON. I was in it, I directed it, it does not matter.

SEAN. Oh, I'm sorry.

ORSON. It was made in 1940, you were probably five.

SEAN. I wasn't born yet.

ORSON. My point is Olivier can't get the money to make a movie of the Scottish play. Larry Olivier has been trying to get the money for a movie of the Scottish play, and he can't raise a dime! Of course what I don't see is why he feels he needs to make a movie of the Scottish play. There already is one. I made it. In 1948, and do you know who I wanted for the Scottish lady? Guess who I wanted for the Scottish lady.

KEN. Who?

ORSON. Vivien.

KEN. Really?

ORSON. You hear that, Sean? You hear the contempt in his voice? Ken hates Vivien Leigh.

KEN. Oh, come now —

ORSON. Hates her!

KEN. I merely —

ORSON. He merely wrote a vicious review of her when she was acting with Larry in the Cleopatra plays, and another when he directed her in *A Streetcar Named Desire*. None of this was Larry's fault, oh, no, although Larry could not stage a cricket match on a very sunny day —

KEN. She was no fucking good, Orson! She had no voice!

ORSON. Oh, Ken. She was kind to me. *(To Sean.)* They have this country place, this ruined abbey founded by King Henry the Fifth — your friend, Sean — and Larry must live there, he would call it Notley, and there is nothing one can say about that, but Vivien made it home. Weekends there would be midnight suppers, for which we dressed, it was like the ball at the *Ambersons*, remember, Ken?

KEN. Yes.

ORSON. The ball at the *Ambersons* was one long shot, Sean —

SEAN. The *Ambersons*?

ORSON. *The Magnificent Ambersons*, and if you've never heard of *Kane* you've certainly never heard of *Ambersons* because that is my most beautiful picture and was therefore ruined by the studio when I was in Brazil.

KEN. Orson —

ORSON. Don't listen to him, Sean. Ken thinks I walked out on the editing of *The Magnificent Ambersons*. And this is my friend! One long shot, Sean, at the ball, down the stairs of this beautiful home, at the turn of that beautiful century, one shot, no cuts, 'til if you ever see it you will be in agony, hoping it will never end, this grace, this loveliness. And there were games, Vivien loved games, she'd make us stay up all night and play charades, and Larry couldn't take it, Larry would go to bed, and I was fat, I thought, " I ought to go to bed, these games will kill me," but then I thought, "Good. Because I'll die in her arms." And Sundays, while Larry and everybody played croquet, she'd set up a table with a typewriter in the garden so I could work on *Chimes at Midnight*, she understood, if I could get a movie made of it, if I could lie on a table in a tavern, as Falstaff, and say. "I'm old, I'm old" on film, then Hollywood might forgive me for having made *Citizen Kane* when I was twenty-six. And Larry wouldn't let me have her for my movie of the Scottish play, because he knows she understands me, and I understand her —

SEAN. Excuse me, Orson —

ORSON. What?

SEAN. The Scottish play?

ORSON. Yes.

SEAN. What's that?

KEN. Careful.

ORSON. You know, Shakespeare's — Scottish play.

SEAN. I never heard of it.

ORSON. Sean, you know the one I mean.

SEAN. The Scottish play?

ORSON. It's not called the Scottish play. People call it that because it's bad luck to say its name inside a theatre, unless you're acting in it and you have to call the title character by name.

SEAN. What's his name.

KEN. Please, Orson. Please.

ORSON. That's my point. You cannot say his name.

SEAN. Whose name?

KEN. Oh, shit.

ORSON. The title character. The Thane. The Thane of Cawdor.

SEAN. Oh! *Macbeth*, you mean.

ORSON. SEAN!

SEAN. Oh! I'm very sorry, Orson.

ORSON. It's all right. It's all right. I mean, this is the moment my life is finally beginning to make sense again, but it's all right, Sean!

SEAN. Oh, what can I do.

ORSON. You can walk around the theatre three times, I think that's what you do. Isn't that what you do, Ken?

KEN. I don't know!

SEAN *(Going.)* I'm going, Orson.

ORSON. Oh, Jesus. Jesus!

KEN. I told you to be careful!

ORSON. Good God, it's just what people say about me, I bring things on myself! — I'll do the play.

KEN. You'll what?

ORSON. I'll direct Olivier in the play.

KEN. Well, thank Christ —

ORSON. What is the play, by the way?

KEN. What?

ORSON. You've never told me what the play is.

KEN. Well, yes, I have, actually —

ORSON. My God, it's *Rhinoceros*.

KEN. Yes.

ORSON. That thing by Ionesco. That thing I saw in Paris.

KEN. Yes.

ORSON. You hate that play.

KEN. To see you flourish once again there is no whoredom I would not undertake.

ORSON. You think this is a good idea for Larry?

KEN. What do you mean?

ORSON. It's modern, that's what I mean. It takes place this side of the fourteenth century.

KEN. That is not fair!

ORSON. Don't tell me what's not fair!

KEN. He played a modern play last year!

ORSON. He did?

KEN. Yes.

ORSON. Had he read it?

KEN. Yes!

ORSON. What was it called?

KEN. *The Entertainer*, and he had a triumph in it.

ORSON. Of course he had a triumph. He always has a triumph. It is his strategy for absolutely everything. Who directed it?

KEN. What?

ORSON. *The Entertainer*. Who? —

KEN. Tony Richardson.

ORSON. Tony Richardson.

KEN. I can't say I care for Tony Richardson.

ORSON. Thank you, Ken. And Larry had a triumph, well, what might happen if he had a strong director, he'd either have a bigger

triumph or a nervous breakdown and either way we'd have a hit!
Oh, Ken! What's this play about? What's the plot?

KEN. What play?

ORSON. *Rhinoceros!*

KEN. I thought you saw it

ORSON. I didn't pay attention. What's the plot?

KEN. It's about a town in which everybody turns into rhinoceroses.

ORSON. And this is —what? — my God, this is a metaphor.
What are you trying to do to me, Ken? A metaphor for what?

KEN. Fascism.

ORSON. Aha. So Larry's going to play a Fascist, this has possi-
bilities.

KEN. No, he's to play the little man, who —

ORSON. WHAT?

KEN. The hero, who stands up against the rest —

ORSON. Larry's going to play the little man? This is a plot, you're
trying to make me look ridiculous.

KEN. If you think it's a plot, why don't I just leave? —

ORSON. STAY HERE! Ken, wait — let's — let's — Whose idea
was this, that Larry play —

KEN. Miss Plowright.

ORSON. Plowright? Joan?

KEN. Yes.

ORSON. I directed Joan Plowright! In *Moby Dick*. You hated her.

KEN. She's grown.

ORSON. Now that she's out of my clutches? Now that Larry's res-
cued her?

KEN. Are they all as neurotic as you, Orson? I really must know.

ORSON. Worse than me. I at least am talented. Why would Larry
let Plowright talk him into this?

KEN. She's had success with other plays by Ionesco.

ORSON. Oh.

KEN. Yes.

ORSON. She's got him by the balls, then. He's weakened.

KEN. I would not count on it.

ORSON. He's out of his depth. I'm a modernist, you know. No
one is aware of that, but I'm a modernist, it's my secret weapon,
wait till you see what I've done for Universal. I think I'm the man
for this, Ken.

KEN. Well, then, set up a meeting, propose yourself.

ORSON. What do you mean, propose myself?

KEN. Well, who else?

ORSON. You.

KEN. I? —

ORSON. It was your idea!

KEN. You expect me to speak to? —

ORSON. Oh, Ken.

KEN. I'll stammer like a fool!

ORSON. You know, you have this habit of revering people. You've got to get over that.

KEN. I revere no one!

ORSON. Talk to him, it'll be the best thing for you.

KEN. Is this some grotesque form of speech therapy?

ORSON. I don't understand. You never stammer around me. Should I resent this? I've always been proud you never stammered around me, I've always thought it was my one undeniable accomplishment —

KEN. Oh, stop that! Stop it!

ORSON. What?

KEN. Stop this relentless, whimsical, revolting self-abnegation when you are our hope! *(Pause.)*

ORSON. I'm sorry.

KEN. So am I. I'll talk to Olivier, I mean of course I'll talk to him.

ORSON. Just talk the way you write, you terrify everybody when you — oh no.

KEN. What?

ORSON. Oh, Ken.

KEN. What?

ORSON. You can't talk to him.

KEN. Why not?

ORSON. What you wrote about Vivien —

KEN. That was ten years ago!

ORSON. You've blown it, Ken. I think we're going to have to forget the whole thing.

KEN. You want to have your work in London again, don't you.

ORSON. I want to have *Chimes at Midnight* in London, not Rhinoceros with Larry Olivier —

KEN. *Chimes at Midnight* has played to empty houses here, and everybody knows it.

ORSON. Empty houses?!

KEN. Orson —

ORSON. You see that? These are rumors!

KEN. Are you seriously saying that it's a rumor that —

ORSON. When and where did you hear the rumor that I've been playing to empty houses?

KEN. I heard it tonight, from the other member of the audience!

ORSON. And I'm sending you as my emissary?

KEN. *(To us.)* But I am his emissary. I have been his emissary since that afternoon I was sixteen, since I saw *Citizen Kane* at a cinema in Birmingham one afternoon —

ORSON. Please don't tell them about *Citizen Kane*. Am I to be remembered for one movie, which I directed from my high chair?

KEN. *(Lights dimming.)* But I must tell them — *(To us.)* — how I saw it every afternoon for the remainder of that week, how I took a different girl each day, how the fifth time I saw it I put on a blindfold, to revel in Orson's use of sound —

ORSON. Don't talk to them anymore, Ken.

KEN. How I wrote that if I had my way Orson would be responsible for the entire American film industry from that moment on —

ORSON. Ken. I can't stand it. *(Pause.)*

KEN. I'm sorry. I'll talk to Olivier.

ORSON. Please, Ken. For me. *(And he leaves. Lights change to ...)*

End of Act One

ACT TWO

Lights bump on, bright. The stage of the Royal Court Theatre in London. It's empty, with a few chairs, maybe a table. Laurence Olivier and Joan Plowright are on the stage. Ken approaches them.

KEN. Sir — Sir Laurence?
LARRY. Mr. Tynan?
KEN. I haven't k-k-k —
LARRY. No — no —
KEN. We had said — said —
LARRY. Six o'clock, yes, and you are punctual. I'm early, of course, it is my curse.
KEN. Well, a critic must be p-p-p-
LARRY. Punctual, yes —
KEN. If nothing else —
LARRY. I once struck a critic across the skull for coming late to one of my productions.
KEN. Ah.
LARRY. It was a play I had directed Vivien in. *The Skin of Our Teeth*. The skin of our fucking teeth indeed, I had directed it to save our marriage. And the leading critic of the day — this was before you had emerged from Oxford, and so the field was still his, poor unsuspecting fellow, now, to be fair, he was punctual for the beginning of the play. But he arrived late for the second act, and that's worse, isn't it, it's not as if he could plead a halting taxi, he was clearly announcing to the audience that he had dawdled at the bar! On Vivien's first night!
KEN. The story is well — well-known —
LARRY. But this was Vivien's first London appearance as half of the Oliviers, I mean, what she faced, poor woman. But I had to do it, I had to put her forth, because, poor thing, I mean, there she was, a bloody film star in their view, those cunts, and here I was, with triumphs suddenly, my *Richard the Third*, my film of *Henry the Fifth* —

26

KEN. *(To us.)* I'm terribly sorry.

LARRY. Lionized at long last thanks in part to you, dear boy, because of the effect you had on those who read the Oxford school paper in those days, although to be brutally honest with you and with myself, it was not just you, you and your fellow critics who gave me a leg up, we must give Herr Hitler a little of the credit, musn't we? —

KEN. Hitler?

LARRY. Well, there he was, across the Channel, wasn't he, at the height of the bloody Blitz, and here I was, on the London stage, as Richard the Third, having a bash at embodying the epitome of Evil. I was bound to provoke the odd frisson, even without the notices, which were very kind, not that kindness has anything to do with it, I know, I know. My point is this. A critic must be punctual, that's all we ask. A brilliant mind, a dazzling prose style like your own, these are the sauce perhaps, but the meal itself, not to batter the poor phrase, is to show up. And in that we are colleagues, aren't we, we are —

JOAN. Darling —

LARRY. What?

JOAN. He said he knows the story.

LARRY. I'm sorry. I'm being very rude. This is Miss Plowright.

JOAN. It's a pleasure.

KEN. I'm — I'm —

LARRY. Could you excuse us for a moment?

KEN. I — of course —

LARRY. Thank you.

KEN. Should I leave?

LARRY. No, no. Just let us talk. I must ask Joan's advice. Vivien's out at Notley alone, poor thing, and I promised I would call her. I mean she wanted me with her, oh I told her I had a meeting, but nothing would do but I must come to Notley, well, she's leaving for New York tomorrow, the first time she'll have acted in New York without me and she's in a bit of a state, I'm sure you sympathize —

KEN. We could postpone the m-m-m —

LARRY. No, no. I am a man of my word. She's doing that play she did here, you know — uh —

JOAN. *Duel of Angels.*

LARRY. Yes, yes. Did you see it, Mr. Tynan?

KEN. Ken —

LARRY. She was very good, I thought.

KEN. Well, she —

LARRY. Well, she's matured. There are those who take her very seriously. *A Streetcar Named Desire?* which I had the honor, really, to direct her in, as I think you will recall —

JOAN. Leave him alone, Larry.

LARRY. I'm pointing out that she's matured. Not that she has not always been superb. Perhaps a little weakness in the voice, as I believe Mr. Tynan has suggested once or twice, but then she can't breathe, can she? She's had TB, of course.

JOAN. *(To Ken.)* She was wonderful in *A Streetcar Named Desire.*

LARRY. You mean the film.

JOAN. That's what I saw.

LARRY. Well, I, of course, did not direct the film.

JOAN. I know.

LARRY. Mr. Kazan was the director of the film.

JOAN. Well, she was very fine.

LARRY. Mr. Kazan changed everything that Vivien and I had worked out.

JOAN. Well, it was very good.

LARRY. What did you like about it, darling?

JOAN. That she was not afraid to let us know that she was out of her mind.

LARRY. Well, I'm sure that's what he wanted, Mr. Kazan. I, of course, had tried to protect her from all that. Well, I loved her.

JOAN. Of course.

LARRY. Isn't this interesting, Mr. Tynan?

KEN. Ken.

LARRY. Darling, should I call her yet?

JOAN. It's just a little after six.

LARRY. I know, it's dusk. Which is her favorite hour, she'll be walking in the garden. I mean, she won't be near the phone.

JOAN. That's what I meant.

LARRY. But that's just it, surely. I can see her trying to decide whether to risk walking in that exquisite garden, at that exquisite hour, which might keep her from hearing the phone, or giving up walking in her garden on her last night there, on the chance that I will call —

JOAN. Why don't you just call her now, don't let it ring long enough for her to hear it if she's in the garden —

LARRY. But, you see, if it's my ring she will hear it!

JOAN. Then let it ring and she'll come in.

LARRY. But then she'll run! She'll be out of breath! Do you want her to be out of breath?

JOAN. No, I don't want her to be out of breath!

LARRY. Then I'm to let her sit beside the phone?

JOAN. Look, call her now, she'll either be beside the phone or she'll be in the garden and when she hears it ring repeatedly she'll know you know she's in the garden and she needn't run, and everybody will be happy.

LARRY. But then she'll want to talk! She likes to talk! In fact, if she's the slightest bit afflicted with the mania, she'll talk incessantly! — *(To Ken.)* — and I know what you're thinking, she has the mania, she talks incessantly, this bugger has not shut up since I arrived! Might I ask you something?

KEN. Of course.

LARRY. Why are you here?

JOAN. Larry!

LARRY. Well, I really don't know why this meeting has been called, and it makes me anxious, rather, it makes me rattle on. I really must know why we're here —

KEN. I want a job.

LARRY. With me?

KEN. Well —

LARRY. What job could I possibly — Good Christ, you don't mean as an actor?

KEN. I — I —

LARRY. Dear boy, you can't speak!

JOAN. Larry —

LARRY. Well, I don't mean to offend, but I do find it saves time to lay out the requirements —

KEN. I have acted, actually —

LARRY. You have?

KEN. In the Guinness *Hamlet*.

LARRY. I hear Alec was dreadful in that *Hamlet*.

KEN. In any case —

LARRY. What is this job?

KEN. At, well, the N-n-n-n —

LARRY. Dear God, the National?

KEN. Yes.

LARRY. The National Theatre of Great Britain?

JOAN. In what capacity, Mr. —

KEN. To — well, advise him —

LARRY. Advise me?

KEN. Yes.

LARRY. About what?

KEN. The — selection —

LARRY. Of what?

KEN. Oh, I don't know. Directors!

LARRY. Directors? People who would direct us?

JOAN. It's a wonderful idea.

LARRY. Why?

JOAN. Because Ken's young.

LARRY. I hate the young.

KEN. Look — is there a play you're about to do right now — before the National —

LARRY. Of course there is. You think we're going to stop acting until the National Theatre has funds? —

KEN. Where are you doing it?

LARRY. Here. At the Royal Court.

KEN. Very good.

LARRY. Thank you so much.

KEN. Tell me what you're — we'll discuss it.

LARRY. Ha! A trial run!

KEN. Yes.

LARRY. The skin bristles.

KEN. I must know the play.

LARRY. We're doing the new Ionesco.

KEN. *Rhinoceros*!

LARRY. What have you to say?

KEN. I say you need a good director.

LARRY. That's brilliant, Ken. I never would have thought of that. Is this the sort of thing I might look forward to were we to work together at the National?

KEN. Yes.

LARRY. Well, who then? Who is your selection? *(Pause.)* Ah, he hesitates. Suspense.

JOAN. Larry, give him a minute.

LARRY. I appreciate your concern, darling. I know you feel that without Ken at my side I will be seen by one and all as a bit of an old fart!

JOAN. I did not say that.

LARRY. But you forget that just last year I did a little thing called *The Entertainer* —

JOAN. I was in it with you.

LARRY. That was modern, one was told.

JOAN. I was in it with you.

LARRY. And you were marvelous. She was marvelous. It was right here at the Royal Court, in case you —

KEN. I remember.

LARRY. Then you will understand why we have already selected our director for *Rhinoceros*.

JOAN. We have?

LARRY. Tony Richardson. Now, not a word of this to anyone, he doesn't know, and he has his film career, of course, he may not want to be seen working a second time with me, a film star from the 1930s! —

KEN. May I say, Tony R-Richardson, is a very bad —

LARRY. Dear boy, if we're to work together you must realize that your opinions carry no weight, no weight at all —

KEN. I —

LARRY. It is your lust for power that intrigues me, really.

JOAN. Then why don't you let him talk?

LARRY. I'm trying! I'm really trying! But Mr. Tynan is brilliant, you see, and if I let him talk I run the risk that he will keep me from the one director who can help me! —

KEN. I am only a critic!

LARRY. Oh, I beg you!—

JOAN. No one can keep you from a thing, Larry! —

LARRY. Tony helps an actor, and how that makes a bad director is beyond my feeble intellect —

KEN. *(Overlap.)* You do not need that sort of help, because you're more than an actor, you're —

LARRY. Stop it.

KEN. You gave me hope! you —

LARRY. Stop it. *(Pause. Ken is silenced.)* There was this moment in *The Entertainer* when I heard my son was dead. At Suez? And there I was, this broken-down vaudevillian, and when I heard I was to crumple and sing a blues song I'd heard a Negress sing once, and Tony said, "None of your tricks now, Larry, none of your shit, you've got to go for it, haven't you, real grief now, none of your faggoty technique, just do it," and I did. Didn't I, Joanie?

JOAN. Yes.

LARRY. Well, you sound hesitant, my darling.

JOAN. No.

31

LARRY. Well, you do a little. And you saw it.

JOAN. Yes, that night. At the dress rehearsal.

LARRY. *(Pause.)* And never again?

JOAN. You made a fine show of it. Every night.

LARRY. A fine show? *(Silence.)* Was Tony terribly disappointed?

JOAN. Darling, it was one moment in a performance none of your peers would have dared try.

KEN. Yes.

LARRY. Was he disappointed?

JOAN. It was one moment, Larry! In a brilliant performance! —.

LARRY. I'm asking you if he was disappointed! —

JOAN. Just a little!

LARRY. Shit!

JOAN. Larry, he's a perceptive man! He saw you'd make a leap, that you had —

LARRY. It was Vivien!

JOAN. And he adores you! He said, "Good Chirst, a great actor who is actually brave!"—

LARRY. Vivien came round!

JOAN. I don't know what you mean.

LARRY. Well, of course Vivien hates this theatre, she hates the Royal Court, because it's modern, she's afraid it will take me right away from her, well, right she is, of course, I think it safe to say the Royal Court will never do a production of *Gone with the Wind*, will it? I mean if she knew I was at the Royal Court right now! —

JOAN. Darling! That night! What did she say?

LARRY. She said, "What the fuck are you doing with that blues song?"

KEN. She did?

LARRY. I would not say another word if I were you.

KEN. What? —

LARRY. It was you who frightened her, as everybody knows.

KEN. I don't know what you —

LARRY. Well, I'll just have to say it, won't I. The review you wrote of the Cleopatra plays I did with her —

JOAN. Oh, call her, Larry! Just call her!

KEN. That was ten years ago!

LARRY. And does that make you think I have forgotten it? Does that make you think you can just come to me with the appalling cheek to say you'd like to work with me? After you wrote that my wife would destroy me if I let her work with me again because I had

32

to stoop to her level? Soon after that she took a lover, an actor — a very fine one, actually — and ran off with him to make a film in Ceylon, in the jungle, from which she had to be brought back in a strait jacket, and since then it's been touch and go, my boy. Touch and go. Let's go, Joan.

JOAN. Mr. Tynan, I really must apologize —

LARRY. I must really end this meeting. It's my fault, it is my weakness, but you see I can't breathe —

JOAN. Are you going to Notley?

LARRY. No, we are going to Brighton. And I am going to run along the beach and breathe! —

JOAN. Ken saved your life.

LARRY. He did what?

KEN. Oh, really, I must —

JOAN. He wrote that you were — dying. Dying artistically is what he meant, but that is dying, isn't it. Isn't it?

LARRY. *(Softly.)* Yes.

JOAN. And he brought you here, here to the Royal Court. He wrote *in the paper* that you must come here, and see what we were on about. He said it might be your salvation. And here you came, the next night. And you came round, and shook our hands, and looked into our eyes, and said how very moved you'd been by the play we had just done —

LARRY. *Roots.*

JOAN. And about the poverty-stricken people we had played so beautifully, and that of course you had to run because you had a Rolls Royce waiting.

LARRY. Well, of course I had a Rolls. I was with Vivien.

JOAN. Must you blame everything on Vivien?

LARRY. No. We fell in love that night, in front of the poor woman.

JOAN. Not I.

LARRY. What?

JOAN. We all despised you.

LARRY. I was the more deceived. *(Pause.)* Christ! Joan!

JOAN. Larry —

LARRY. Darling —

JOAN. Don't.

LARRY. I know.

JOAN. No, listen. You came back —

LARRY. Forgive me —

JOAN. You came back here to do *The Entertainer*, and you rolled up your sleeves, physically, literally, and you were new. And none of this —

LARRY. I was new because of you.

JOAN. Would have been possible but for an article by this man, in his concern for you.

LARRY. I wish I were young again!

JOAN. You are. But let him tell you who he thinks should direct you.

LARRY. Mr. Tynan?

KEN. Y-y-yyyes? —

LARRY. Have you noticed how I'm dressed?

KEN. Oh, I —

LARRY. What do you think?

KEN. Well, I had not expected you to look like a — like a —

LARRY. Like what.

KEN. A banker.

LARRY. It's all right. Of course you didn't. 'Til now my style was velvet jackets. Vivien would buy me velvet jackets. And now, look, beneath this plain jacket — *(He removes his suit jacket.)* one finds a work shirt. I am a simple man, really. Or, no, complex, but allied finally with a woman of abiding, beautiful simplicity. Joanie. I can't tell you the — well, the relief, and relief, one finds, can be the deepest of the passions.

KEN. M-mm — might we discuss the —

LARRY. Good Christ, he is relentless.

JOAN. I think he's been the soul of patience.

LARRY. She's read your stuff, you know.

KEN. Who?

LARRY. Joanie.

JOAN. Larry.

KEN. My? —

LARRY. Stuff.

JOAN. With pleasure and edification.

LARRY. I mean your notices of her.

JOAN. I told him not to mention this, of course.

LARRY. Joan, be honest with the man.

KEN. I hope I've not seemed disrespectful.

LARRY. Disrespectful?!

JOAN. He means the Ionesco one-acts.

LARRY. It wasn't just the Ionesco one-acts.

34

KEN. But I'm sure I found you staggering in the Ionesco one-acts.

JOAN. I think you were staggered in the first one. In the second, I believe, you regained your footing.

LARRY. Mr. Tynan never loses that for very long.

KEN. I-I-I must confess something.

LARRY. Must you?

KEN. I don't care for Ionesco.

LARRY. You don't care for Ionesco?

KEN. Yes, and that M-miss Plowright was able to stagger me for fully half —

LARRY. Surely your job is to separate these things.

JOAN. Are you questioning Mr. Tynan's professionalism?

KEN. Ken! —

LARRY. I am coming to your rescue, darling! You forget I am a knight! I have been knighted! And a knight is supposed to protect the lady that he loves, isn't he.

JOAN. No.

LARRY. All right, then, I'll forget that he alluded to your "agonized inadequacy."

KEN. Her what?

JOAN. Oh, Christ, Larry!

KEN. Did I say "agonized inadequacy?"

JOAN. When I worked with Orson.

KEN. Oh! Oh, yes, in M-m-m-

LARRY. *Moby Dick*. Of course now you're going to tell me you don't care for Orson Welles, the only genius we have in our line! —

KEN. He is my friend!

LARRY. Then ask your friend why he'd expose a gifted young actress in his care to the charge of "agonized inadequacy" —

KEN. You know, if you must read reviews, and, even worse, remember them, you must read them with more intelligence.

LARRY. *(After quite a pause.)* I beg your pardon?

KEN. I think you read them with that animal alertness that is the hallmark of your acting. I think you read them, well, downwind. You must read them carefully.

LARRY. How carefully must one read a phrase like "agonized inadequacy"?

KEN. Carefully enough to understand that agonized inadequacy is hopeful. Complacent inadequacy is not. Miss Plowright has never been complacent.

JOAN. Joan.

LARRY. Your selection, it would seem, is Mr. Welles.

KEN. What?

LARRY. I know he's your friend, but tell me why I need to work with him.

KEN. How did you guess?

LARRY. Animal alertness. Orson's in Dublin, isn't he.

JOAN. Doing the Falstaff play.

LARRY. Ah, yes.

KEN. Yes.

LARRY. That thing.

KEN. Yes.

LARRY. How's it going.

KEN. Well —

LARRY. Well, there it is, you see.

KEN. I —

LARRY. He's been working on that thing since he was at that school. What was that school?

KEN. The Todd School for Boys —

LARRY. I'm sorry. Did you say the Todd School for Boys?

KEN. Yes.

LARRY. I rest my case.

KEN. He wants to make a film of it.

LARRY. Then let him.

KEN. He can't.

LARRY. The money.

KEN. Yes.

LARRY. Orson Welles can't get the money for a film. Orson Welles, in his prime years —

KEN. One hears you can't get the money to film the Scottish play.

LARRY. Mr. Tynan —

KEN. Even with Miss Leigh!

LARRY. Mr. Tynan —

JOAN. You're going to make a film with Vivien?

LARRY. She's a star, darling. And, well, investors — Good work, Ken! Really smashing work!

JOAN. Larry, who are you using?

LARRY. In the film?

JOAN. In your life. Are you using Vivien or are you using me?

LARRY. Well, both, actually! I mean it's not what you —

JOAN. I've worked with Orson. You have not.

LARRY. Well, I know him, too, and Orson reminds me just a bit

36

of Vivien, if you must know.

KEN. I beg your pardon?

LARRY. Hadn't thought of that one, had you. Either of you! Of course Orson's more deliberate than Vivien, I mean Orson goes swimming and develops a cramp, having already summoned his supporters to the shore!

JOAN. Larry —

LARRY. I mean Orson fails, doesn't he. He fails. And, Ken, I don't think you and I can work together at the National, you seem to be a little sentimental about rescuing lost souls. In print of course you have great value and I look forward to many years of reading you, and I urge you to be ruthless with me, as you have with my dear, tormented wife —

JOAN. CALL HER!

LARRY. I — really, I —

JOAN. Ken and I will be at the pub.

LARRY. It's interesting you say that Ken and I will be at the pub.

JOAN. It's interesting that you should find that interesting.

LARRY. All right, I'll call her. But when I do I'm going to break it off with her. I'm going to tell her everything.

JOAN. That is insane.

LARRY. What's been going on this past year is insane.

JOAN. If you tell her she'll suffer an episode.

LARRY. She'll suffer an episode no matter what I do. You know nothing, any of you, of what it's like to live with someone who will suffer an episode if one so much as gets a good review.

KEN. My mother died insane —

LARRY. Well, I am grieved to hear it! *(Pause.)* I'm sorry. Died insane, dear, what a dreadful thing. What a dreadful thing. What should I do? I don't know what to do.

JOAN. Ask Ken.

LARRY. *(Pause.)* Ken?

KEN. I-I — Break it off.

LARRY. Break it off. With Vivien. *(Ken is silent.)* Darling?

JOAN. *(Pause.)* Yes.

LARRY. *(Goes to phone and dials.)* Thames 1-5-6, please.

JOAN. And, please, Ken and I will go to the pub.

LARRY. No.

JOAN. I want you to take your time, darling.

LARRY. Don't go.

JOAN. You're going to break it off with her!

KEN. Perhaps I should go —

LARRY. Don't go. Either of you.

VIVIEN. Hello? *(Vivien has entered, ringing phone in hand, at Notley. There is no set for Notley; there are lights, though.)*

LARRY. Hello, darling.

VIVIEN. Larry.

LARRY. You don't sound out of breath. I was afraid you'd be in the garden and have to dash in.

VIVIEN. I was in the garden.

LARRY. Oh. Good, then. I am shutting my eyes and imagining how lovely it is.

VIVIEN. I'm going to miss it.

LARRY. Of course. But then New York will be over, and it will go well for you, and you can have the summer there, which is my favorite time of the year at Notley, and we can bask in it, and — *(He stops. Pause.)*

VIVIEN. Why did you pause?

LARRY. I — I'm just — so excited for you. New York, on your own. Are you excited, darling?

VIVIEN. More frightened, actually —

LARRY. There is nothing to be frightened —

VIVIEN. Can you hurry up here?

LARRY. Darling —

VIVIEN. I'll have them put out a light supper, and some wine —

LARRY. You are marvelous in that play, Vivien.

VIVIEN. I'm not frightened about the play.

LARRY. But there is nothing else to be frightened of, my —

VIVIEN. Do you remember the last time I was in New York?

LARRY. Well, when we took the Cleopatra plays there after London —

VIVIEN. That was ten years ago.

LARRY. And what a ten years it has been, hasn't it, and you have come so far. Well, we both have. And I know this will be your first time on the New York stage without me, without being half of the Oliviers, which must be bloody boring —

VIVIEN. The last time I was in New York was with you, just last year.

LARRY. I don't —

VIVIEN. When you took *The Entertainer* there.

LARRY. Of course! Of course! You came for the opening, such madness —

38

VIVIEN. And you had a run-through and every actor in New York was asked, and you were inspired and we all rushed round to tell you and you would not hear of it. You said, "Tonight means nothing to me. Because I did not know what I was doing." But I've been wondering. Since I'm going to New York, why don't I try to do what you did that one night, except why don't I try to do it every night, just not know what I'm doing —

LARRY. Oh, darling —

VIVIEN. What?

LARRY. You musn't.

VIVIEN. Why not?

LARRY. Because you know, darling, how much it means to you, the regularity of it —

VIVIEN. Larry —

LARRY. The reassuring rhythm in the theatre of knowing exactly what it is that you must do each night —

VIVIEN. But that's because I'm crazy, Larry.

LARRY. Put it however you wish to put it —

VIVIEN. There is no wish involved here —

LARRY. Darling, I'm telling you this for your own good —

VIVIEN. I know you are!

LARRY. And, really, that's why you're so exquisite on the stage, because everything is held in place so carefully —

VIVIEN. Marlon Brando changes it every time.

LARRY. Well, then.

VIVIEN. He never knows what he's going to do.

LARRY. I think perhaps he gives off that illusion.

VIVIEN. When we were filming *Streetcar* he never did the same thing twice. Kazan adored it, that's the kind of director he is.

LARRY. You've told me this.

VIVIEN. And what I never told you is that I'd amuse myself, thinking "Larry would go mad." When you directed it here, in London, in fucking London, you used to tell us what to do precisely, at every moment, and not to change, never to change —

LARRY. I did this for you, of course —

VIVIEN. I'd add one gesture, you'd say, "Well, a little Baroque this evening, aren't we?"

LARRY. I think you're remembering inaccurately —

VIVIEN. I remember everything you've ever done!

LARRY. Well, then perhaps you'll remember that everything I've done for many years has been to protect you, because I know better than anyone —

VIVIEN. I'm going to try it, Larry.

LARRY. *(Flares.)* Well, good, then! Have a bash at it, I say! *(Pause.)*

VIVIEN. What — what —

LARRY. What is it, darling.

VIVIEN. What wine would you like tonight?

LARRY. Darling, I have this bloody meeting here in town. As I've told you.

VIVIEN. Where is this meeting?

LARRY. What?

VIVIEN. The meeting.

LARRY. Oh! Oh, its —

VIVIEN. Oh, really, I'm not coming there, I'm not going to track you down.

LARRY. Of course! I didn't —

VIVIEN. I just want to know where you are.

LARRY. I'm in an office somewhere. I'm not even sure —

VIVIEN. Larry —

LARRY. I mean, I was brought here. I'm afraid I was abducted, actually! —

VIVIEN. You've never been abducted in your life —

LARRY. I'm sorry if I got a little cross just now. It's just, your telling me about that run-through in New York does make me think of when you came to see the play in London, the first night I ever played it in front of any audience, when you came round and told me I'd disgraced myself —

VIVIEN. I never said you had disgraced yourself.

LARRY. You said, "What the fuck do you think you're doing with that blues song?" And —

VIVIEN. Larry —

LARRY. What?

VIVIEN. What were you doing with that blues song?

LARRY. Tony told me to do it! And I did! And I'm afraid that's what happens every time I just do something, I'm afraid that you all say "Oh, Larry, musn't do that, no," no, all the rest of you can do that, but, no, Larry is the captain, isn't he? —

VIVIEN. That is not what I meant!

LARRY. And so I was never able to do it again, I acceded to your wishes, darling, as I try to do, and once again I was severely compromised —

VIVIEN. You bastard!

LARRY. And I'm afraid that many people were quite disappointed, Tony, the other members of the cast —

VIVIEN. I was trying to protect the other members of the cast!

LARRY. Are you saying they need to be protected from me?

VIVIEN. There were people who were acting from their hearts that night! That — Brenda — your wife, that marvelous Joan Plowright, and you just had to wipe them out, you had to hurl yourself against a wall and pretend that you were Bessie Smith! Bessie Smith! Do you know the first thing about poor Bessie Smith?

LARRY. *(Alarmed.)* Vivien —

VIVIEN. She bled to death! You bastard! She bled to death because they would not treat her at a Southern hospital! Do you know what that feels like! Do you know what it feels like to be left to die, to be put into a strait jacket? —

LARRY. I'm coming out there.

VIVIEN. No!

LARRY. I'll be there in no time.

VIVIEN. Larry —

LARRY. Of course there may be traffic.

VIVIEN. You have your meeting.

LARRY. You don't want me to come out, then.

VIVIEN. It's just that —

LARRY. You're afraid of me.

VIVIEN. Larry, it's just that I'm afraid I feel the mania a bit, and I know that frightens you.

LARRY. You mean you're afraid I'm going to hit you.

VIVIEN. Larry, listen to me. That was my fault. I was crazy. You don't understand just how it is —

LARRY. How what is?

VIVIEN. An attack of mania. It is impossible to sleep, and terrifying if anybody else can sleep —

LARRY. Are you saying, then, that I don't understand? —

VIVIEN. I think you just can't understand sometimes that I am crazy, that's —

LARRY. That's quite a thing to say, after all that —

VIVIEN. And if you could I think you'd be much happier, because you would not take me quite so seriously. You wouldn't feel this guilt, which makes you such a bore. What have I done to you, I sometimes wonder. My life has a moral, it really has a moral. If you're manic-depressive never marry the minister's son. Even if he is the sexiest man in the world.

LARRY. Sexier than Brando?

VIVIEN. Do stop.

LARRY. Did you and Brando —

VIVIEN. Oh, well, I'm fairly sure I would remember that.

LARRY. Because I know you and Kazan —

VIVIEN. That what? We what?

LARRY. Darling, in New York one night I went to Sardi's and Kazan was at a table with the actors from whatever naturalistic thing he was directing then, and I heard him say to them, "You see that man? I fucked his wife."

VIVIEN. He said that?

LARRY. And I moved on, not having heard, you know, and I thought, it happened on the film of *Streetcar*, and you would never have been in that film if I had not directed you in it on the stage, that marvelous play about, I have to say, a nymphomaniac —

VIVIEN. She is not a nymphomaniac!

LARRY. Which I took on after I'd been asked to join a club with Winston Churchill! I had everything to lose!

VIVIEN. Oh, now you're saying I kept you from Winston Churchill!

LARRY. And then to hear it said in public that he fucked you? He fucked you, darling!

VIVIEN. Well, it's a dirty job but somebody's got to do it.

LARRY. Oh, darling —

VIVIEN. Darling, how do you know he even meant it? He likes to excite his actors, as I told you.

LARRY. I am an animal onstage, and cannot be an animal everywhere —

VIVIEN. What are you wearing?

LARRY. What?

VIVIEN. Right now. What are you wearing?

LARRY. What am I wearing?

VIVIEN. Please. Tell me.

LARRY. Well, the — well, the velvet jacket —

VIVIEN. Lovely.

JOAN. We really must go.

LARRY. *(Hissing.)* No!

VIVIEN. Who's that?

LARRY. One of the people I'm meeting with.

VIVIEN. He sounds tough.

LARRY. He is.

42

VIVIEN. Are they listening to this?

LARRY. Someone just popped in to see how long I'd — it's all right —

VIVIEN. What is this meeting about?

LARRY. Oh — you know.

VIVIEN. No, I don't know.

LARRY. Well, since you must know I'm trying to get the money for our film —

VIVIEN. What?

LARRY. And I didn't want to mention it because I know how you can get your hopes up —

VIVIEN. Oh, Larry, who is going to put money in that film?

LARRY. Darling, I can get the money.

VIVIEN. Let me go to New York! Let me get on with my stage work! Let me be something other than an aging film star! —

LARRY. I can get the money! You forget that you're a legendary film actress.

VIVIEN. Mary Pickford is a legendary film actress, but I don't see anybody putting up the money to star her in a movie of *Macbeth*! —

LARRY. VIVIEN! Vivien, why did you say that?

VIVIEN. Why did I say —

LARRY. The name of that character, the title of that play!

VIVIEN. Are you out of your mind?

LARRY. I am not out of my mind, you know how dangerous —

VIVIEN. Darling, you are actually upset about this! —

LARRY. Don't you know me at all?

VIVIEN. Larry, all right, I'm sorry I said it, but what does it matter?

LARRY. What does it matter?

VIVIEN. It only matters if you're in a theatre when you say it, and I'm not in a theatre right now —

LARRY. But I am! *(Pause.)* I mean — *(Long pause.)*

VIVIEN. Where are you?

LARRY. At the Royal Court.

VIVIEN. Yes.

LARRY. I'll come out.

VIVIEN. Are you going to do another play there?

LARRY. Yes.

VIVIEN. What?

LARRY. *Rhinoceros.*

VIVIEN. That one we saw in Paris?

43

LARRY. Yes.

VIVIEN. You hated that play.

LARRY. Well, you know, though, it was something new, wasn't it.

VIVIEN. You hated *Rhinoceros*. We laughed about it.

LARRY. Darling, I'm playing the one who stands alone at the end, who refuses to turn into a rhino like the rest of them, which is marvelous when one begins to delve because until that point, if you'll remember, he keeps saying "I'm afraid of life," so —

VIVIEN. "I'm afraid of life"?

LARRY. Well, it's a challenge for me, isn't it. And, as I say, you know me —

VIVIEN. A challenge?!

LARRY. Yes, and —

VIVIEN. You have no idea what that is, to be afraid of life.

LARRY. How dare you say that to me.

VIVIEN. Larry?

LARRY. What?

VIVIEN. The girl is going to have to be so charming. In the play.

LARRY. I — yes. Yes. That's very smart, you're very smart about —

VIVIEN. I love you.

LARRY. And I — the same —

VIVIEN. Has someone popped his head back in again?

LARRY. Yes.

VIVIEN. Shall I let you go, then?

LARRY. I am so very proud of you.

VIVIEN. I'll be back in the summer. We can have a summer here together. And we needn't have people out on weekends, I know how that exhausts you, and you're going to be exhausted, oh my poor darling, if you've just been playing someone who's afraid of life. *(Silence.)* Larry?

LARRY. I — I —

VIVIEN. Au revoir. *(She hangs up. He hangs up. Silence.)*

JOAN. Larry?

LARRY. I — *(Silence. Suddenly he embraces her desperately. She resists at first, then accepts. Finally he moves to Ken.)* Well, Ken, I let you down. I did not break if off with Vivien.

KEN. I — it's not my — my —

LARRY. I'm sorry I was so harsh about Orson. He is your friend, and I respect how you look after him, I do. God knows he's gifted. Well. He's a gift. Yes. And we must treasure these people, encourage them, really, even if, particularly if, they flail about. And even though I do think I've helped Vivien these past few years — I like to think that — I just don't trust myself as much as I would like about this sort of thing. So what I suppose I want to know is, do you trust me? Do you trust me with your friend?

KEN. Of course.

LARRY. Then let's hire him, shall we? Good. Good, then. Joan, your wish is my command. We're going to hire Orson.

JOAN. Good.

LARRY. Good, then. Well, then, a good night's work. Let's go to that pub. *(He leads them off. Ken breaks away, and is left alone with Vivien. He looks at her: She of course does not see him. Then:)*

KEN. *(To us.)* Intermission. *(He goes off.)*

End of Act Two

ACT THREE

The stage of the Royal Court. Perhaps part of the set for Rhinoceros *is in place. Ken and Orson are there. They are tense, silent. After a moment Ken comes forward and speaks to us.*

KEN. We're two weeks in. It's been — it's been — I must say I've been harsh sometimes about things I have reviewed. Particularly if it's been the work of people I admire. I suppose I've thought if they're capable of greatness they should bloody well achieve it! That surely all they need is a cheerfully administered humiliation, as by a brisk, demented fourth-form rugby coach, to lash them on. What I see now is that they've done anything of any worth at all is a miraculous achievement. Because they are in fact insane. *(Orson gets up, leaves the stage.)* He hates it when I talk like this. But then I talk too much when I'm around him. I've followed him for years all over Europe like a yapping hound pursuing a large, drifting air balloon, as he floated about, after his exile from Hollywood in 1948, trying to raise money for his films himself, from Hungarians and Middle Easterners, at long dinners in hotel dining rooms in Venice and Madrid, in which he told them of his dreams of filming *Don Quixote* or of finishing his filming of *Othello*, and they asked him what it was like to have sex with Rita Hayworth. Or, if they mentioned his work at all, why he hadn't made a decent film since *Citizen Kane*. And he believes that that's what I think, too, which it is not. I try to tell him he's a living genius, and once one is called a living genius one only exists to disappoint. I tell him the only reason that they miss those early works is that they want to be that age again, discovering him, discovering the world, but, wait, I tell him, when he's dead they'll see the value of everything he's done —
ORSON. *(Reenters.)* And this is meant to cheer me up.
KEN. *(To us.)* Well, there you see that, I can't help him —
ORSON. Stop trying, Ken. Why am I early?
KEN. This is in response to complaints that you have made that every morning we have come to find Larry and Joan already here.

ORSON. What do I care whether Larry and Joan are —

KEN. At which point you whisper that they clearly got here early so that he could re-direct her!

ORSON. I'll tell you what's happening. I'm directing Joan to be a modern girl and he wants the girl to be like Vivien. This is messy, Ken. I hate mess!

SEAN. *(Enters.)* Orson, Ken, they're here.

LARRY. *(Off.)* Well, what have we here?

ORSON. Good morning, Larry.

LARRY. *(Enters with Joan.)* We're early, are we.

ORSON. Is that all right?

LARRY. Of course it's all right.

ORSON. It's just I'm so excited about what we're doing that I couldn't wait.

LARRY. Very good.

ORSON. I mean, I can go back to the hotel and sleep a little longer if you —

LARRY. Not at all. It's just —

ORSON. What?

LARRY. Well, it's just this is the moment in the day when Joanie and I —

ORSON. When you what?

LARRY. Get our bearings —

ORSON. What bearings?

JOAN. Here, Orson.

ORSON. What?

JOAN. Scones and jam.

ORSON. But these are for you and Larry.

JOAN. And now you're here we'll all share, won't we. Ken?

KEN. Oh! No! N-n-n — *(He coughs.)*

JOAN. Ken, sit down with us and eat.

LARRY. I'm glad you're here, dear boy, because there's something I wanted to discuss.

ORSON. About what?

LARRY. Well, about Joanie's performance —

ORSON. You want to talk about Joan's performance?

LARRY. You seem to be telling her things —

ORSON. Whatever made me think I could do that?

JOAN. I went to a new shop for these scones.

ORSON. What? You did what?

JOAN. A new shop. I like these better. You're in luck, Orson.

47

ORSON. Am I? Am I in luck?

JOAN. Yes.

ORSON. I'd been beginning to wonder if that would ever be true again.

LARRY. Well, I know that feeling!

ORSON. You do?

LARRY. Well, I know, the Olivier career looks effortless to all of you.

ORSON. It does, yes.

JOAN. Well, everything looks easy to everybody else.

LARRY. Well, the ease of Orson's rise appalled most people! You can't imagine the effect —

JOAN. Are you saying I'm too young?

ORSON. I think he's saying that anybody under forty is too young.

LARRY. I wasn't saying that.

KEN. I think what's wrong here is that Orson feels, Sir Laurence, that you ruined him in Hollywood in 1948! *(There is an appalled silence.)*

LARRY. Orson —

ORSON. Ken!

KEN. I thought it might be best to clear the air.

ORSON. Why don't we just get started?

LARRY. No, just a moment —

ORSON. No, let's get started, I shouldn't be eating this, Joan, it's very kind of you but I shouldn't, I mean, I'm very fat!

JOAN. Whatever you want, Orson.

ORSON. I think we seem to be in disagreement, at least Larry and I seem to, about this scene between you, so if we could —

LARRY. Dear boy, I must clear this up.

ORSON. There's nothing to clear up. I'm a sick man, maddened by decades of failure, who says things. So! Sean! Set up that scene between Larry and Joan.

SEAN. Which one, Orson.

ORSON. The last one! The only one they've got!

SEAN. But they're together many times in the play.

ORSON. But not alone! This is the first time they're alone, haven't you been watching? Or have you been dreaming about meeting Abbott and Costello?

SEAN. I'm not in the rehearsals —

JOAN. Perhaps we ought to wait for the stage manager. It's dreadfully early.

ORSON. It's dawn is what it is! It's dawn!

SEAN. I mean, I go for tea.

KEN. This is my fault.

SEAN. I could go back to Dublin.

KEN. Everything's my fault.

ORSON. Will you stop smoking? *(Grabs cigarette from him.)*

JOAN. Sean! Let me show you the arrangement.

LARRY. Shall we start from where we're left alone, then. What is your will, maestro?

ORSON. Start. Just start.

LARRY. Very well. Now, that is at the end of the play, Sean, for future reference. Might I just ask one thing, Orson?

ORSON. Is it about Joan's performance or your own?

LARRY. Mine, of course.

ORSON. Because you mentioned Joan's a moment ago.

LARRY. I know I did, old cock, and I feel very properly chastised. *(Pause; all stop their activities.)*

ORSON. Thank you, Larry.

LARRY. Well, then. He's alone with Daisy for the first time. My question is, what should I do?

ORSON. What?

LARRY. It's just that in the last few days you've changed what Joanie's doing and I feel a bit confused.

ORSON. I thought you said this was about your own performance.

LARRY. I've passed a sleepless night.

KEN. Might I say something?

ORSON. Shut up, Ken.

LARRY. I've been trying to work out a new way to play my fellow to mesh with what you'd like for Joanie, and I enlist your help, old boy.

ORSON. How do you feel about this, Joan?

LARRY. Yes, yes, of course, ask Joan.

ORSON. How do you feel?

JOAN. You seem to see this girl as pretty hard.

LARRY. Well, that's just it, you see —

JOAN. And I see what Orson means.

LARRY. You do.

JOAN. Well, I've come to Ionesco before you, of course —

LARRY. Before Orson, too, of course —

JOAN. Before you or Orson, so I'm in a position, really, to see Orson's point.

LARRY. Well, I'll just have to muddle through, then, which is perfectly all right!

JOAN. On the other hand we share the stage, so we must try to work it out.

LARRY. I see. Good. Good!

JOAN. Did I answer you, Orson?

ORSON. Yes, you did.

LARRY. I'm willing to concede I may have been going at it all wrong. I mean, she's in his flat for the first time, and it's possible I've been a little ardent. I mean, that film I did with Vivien, *That Hamilton Woman*, do you know it, Orson?

ORSON. Yes.

LARRY. Well, I know, it's romantic stuff, well, it was made during the war, it was made to help us get through the war, it was Winston's favorite film! He adored Vivien from that day on! ... *(Pause.)* Where was I? Where was I, Joanie?

JOAN. I don't know.

LARRY. Forgive me. The only point I was trying to make is that that was the last time in my work I've been alone with a woman, and I was Lord Nelson after all, so perhaps my sense of this is a little bit askew. If I might just think through this a moment, ploddingly, ploddingly, I am not a clever boy. So. We're alone. And I know she's only in my flat because she knew my rival was in my flat. But now he's off to join his fellow citizens as a rhinoceros, and Daisy and my fellow are the only ones left in town who are maintaining human form, which is really a moment of some opportunity. And my fellow must seize it, and he does not know what to do. Which I can't grasp at all. I mean, when one's chance does come, one lunges for it, isn't that true, Orson.

ORSON. *(On guard.)* Yes.

LARRY. I mean, you lunged for things, didn't you, in your youth? One remembers!

ORSON. I lunge for them now.

LARRY. Well, then, explain to me why this fellow, when his opportunity arises, is so, well, inept.

ORSON. Maybe he's lost his way.

LARRY. But — forgive me — how could a man who has everything before him lose his way?

ORSON. I don't know. Maybe he — *(Pause.)* Look, it's Theatre of the Absurd.

LARRY. I'm not sure that's an answer, old cock —

ORSON. Sean?

SEAN. Yes, Orson.

ORSON. Give me a sandwich.

LARRY. Dear boy, I don't know what to do. Now, I know, you need a sandwich! —

ORSON. I see your problem, Larry. It's the room. The way you've set the room up while I was eating my scone. It's orderly. This place should be a mess. *(Suddenly, aggressively, he begins to mess it up.)*

LARRY. What are you doing?

ORSON. *(Overturning.)* I'm showing you the mess you live in.

LARRY. You are violating everything I know about my fellow!

ORSON. You said you didn't understand your fellow.

LARRY. I can't be responsible for everything I say!

ORSON. Well, you said you don't know what to do, so I'm giving you something, which is to clean up!

LARRY. Clean up? How do I clean up?

ORSON. You're asking me how to clean up? You think I have the slightest idea how to clean up?

LARRY. Well, you are the director.

ORSON. All right, Larry.

LARRY. I mean, since you ask, I don't really associate you with cleaning up —

ORSON. I said, all right! I'll tell you what to do!

LARRY. Splendid!

ORSON. Dust!

LARRY. All right. Good, good. Dust. *(He starts to, stops.)* How do I dust, though? It's clear my fellow's never dusted. How does one dust, never having dusted?

ORSON. I don't know.

LARRY. It's all right, Orson. It's all right. Dust. That's good. But what to do, that's all. And of course he musn't let her see him dusting, she's looking out the window, so I know, I'll dust covertly. *(He does.)* But how do I hold the dust cloth? Balled up? I could mop my brow — oh, no, one is only fifty-three, and one is mired in cliché! But it doesn't matter. It does not matter. So here I am, I'm dusting, I say, "Oh, Daisy." "Oh, Daisy." *(Silence.)*

SEAN. *(On book.)* "Oh, Daisy, I never knew" —

LARRY. Shut up! I know the line! "Oh, Daisy, I never knew" *(Tries to laugh.)* There, you see? "I never knew" *(Pause.)* Good Christ, the lines. This is new. Well, I don't know what to do, that's all. Quite right, Orson, very good, I must know what to do —

ORSON. Let it hang, Larry.

LARRY. What?

ORSON. The cloth. Keep it balled up, then when you go to talk to her, just let it open, without realizing it in your, you know, passion, and the dirt will fall out on the floor —

LARRY. Yes, yes, farce stuff. Good. "Oh, Daisy, I never knew" — "I never knew" — *(He lets the cloth fall open.)* Oh, well, I don't believe it. Did anybody in this room believe that? That I let it fall open in my passion? Sean, did you believe that?

SEAN. No.

ORSON. Sean!

LARRY. No, no, he speaks the truth! How can I let it fall open in my passion when there is no passion, and how can there be passion when the girl is hard? I mean, it was a lovely idea, Orson but, you see, it's just not possible, is it, since —

ORSON. Larry, forget the cloth.

LARRY. Oh, dear boy, I shall try —

ORSON. *(Takes the cloth.)* Forget it.

LARRY. *(Tries to grab it back.)* Give me back the cloth.

ORSON. I don't want you unhappy.

LARRY. Dear boy, I don't want to fight.

ORSON. Who's fighting? I'm not fighting.

LARRY. I'm trying to be friends! I am, I am! —

ORSON. I know that! Take the cloth!

LARRY. *(Takes it.)* Forgive me, forgive me, everyone. Mea culpa, mea culpa. "Oh, Daisy, I never knew" — *(He stops.)* What are the words, please.

SEAN. "Oh, Daisy, I never knew I could feel so much emotion."

LARRY. "Oh, Daisy, I never knew I could feel so much" — *(He stops.)* "so much" —

SEAN. "Emotion."

LARRY. Stop it!

ORSON. Sean?

SEAN. Yes, Orson.

ORSON. Leave the room.

LARRY. *(As Sean leaves.)* Thank you, Orson.

ORSON. It's all right.

LARRY. I mean, he terrifies me.

ORSON. So. "Oh, Daisy" Ken, say the lines in case he can't —

KEN. But I can't —

LARRY. "Oh, Daisy, I never could" — Well, yes. Yes, Orson, quite right, we must lose the cloth. But what to do? We must find what

52

to do. Very well, I must get her attention, musn't I. She's looking out the window at my rival, well, then, I'll bring her tea, yes, move the table over to the window, move the chair that she may sit in it while gazing at my rival, yes — *(He's doing all this.)* "Oh, Daisy" … "Oh, Daisy" … *(Silence.)* Fuck me in the tits!

KEN. "Oh, Daisy, I n-n-n — "

LARRY. Will you say the fucking line? Oh, dear. Oh, dear. You can't say the fucking line. I'm sorry. This is a nightmare. It's all right, Ken. I don't need the line, in fact — may I speak frankly? — I don't want the line. And do you know why? Because I don't know how to say the line. I mean, this play is set in France. It's set in fucking France. How do I speak any of the lines, that is the question we must face. Do you seriously want me to play a French man in a French town speaking English in a bad French accent? This is ridiculous. And why do I bring her tea if we're in France? It means nothing, it says nothing.

ORSON. Larry, I'll set the play in England.

LARRY. What do you mean, you'll set the play in England? The play is set in France. There was no Fascism in England, thank you very much.

ORSON. I'll set it in England if we can just move on —

LARRY. Move on. Well, there it is, you see. Never mind the little people. But it's not my business, is it, I'm not the director, let's just carry on.

JOAN. If you looked at me.

LARRY. What?

JOAN. If you looked at me, the lines you're meant to speak might come to you.

LARRY. Very well, very well. Good, good. "Oh, Daisy" — "Oh, Daisy" —

JOAN. It's "Oh, Daisy, I never knew I could feel so much emotion," and you're not looking at me.

LARRY. How can you tell? Orson has you looking out the window. How can you tell I'm not looking at you if you're not looking at me?

JOAN. I can just tell.

LARRY. "Oh, Daisy, I never knew I could feel so much emotion" —

JOAN. What are you looking at?

LARRY. I'm trying to find out why my fellow feels so much emotion!

JOAN. Who are you looking at, Larry? I mean, in your mind's eye!

LARRY. My mind's eye? I have no mind anymore, how can I tell you what I'm seeing in my mind's eye? I'm not as smart as you are, darling, not as smart as Ken, or Orson certainly, or Sean, or you, well, of course I'm not as smart as you, I'm old-fashioned, you see, well, of course I am, I mean I'm moved by *Gone with the Wind*! Oh, now, I didn't mean that.

JOAN. I think we ought to take a break.

LARRY. No!

JOAN. We'll have our tea. *(Calls.)* Sean!

LARRY. Oh, darling, I beg you, don't call Sean!

JOAN. Sean! *(As Sean appears.)* Pour the tea.

LARRY. *(As Sean starts to.)* One moment. One moment, please. Very well. Sean is in the room. Welcome, Sean. But we are not to take a break.

KEN. I think I need to say that progress is —

ORSON. I think so, too. You think so, Joan?

JOAN. Of course I think so. I just want some tea.

LARRY. Darling, we must work.

JOAN. Sugar, Larry?

ORSON. You think we're making progress, Larry?

LARRY. Progress? Sugar?

ORSON. Give him some tea, Joan.

JOAN. I'm just trying.

LARRY. I don't want tea, I am a giant in chains.

ORSON. I know how you feel. Oh, I know how you feel.

LARRY. Of course I did not forge my chains myself. Forgive me, forgive me, never mind.

ORSON. I hear you're going to run the National.

LARRY. Who told you that? I said, no tea!

KEN. May we get back to work?

ORSON. Because I'm offering you *Chimes at Midnight* at the National.

LARRY. This tea is piss, and what the fuck is *Chimes at Midnight*?

JOAN. The Falstaff thing.

LARRY. Ah, yes.

ORSON. Yes.

LARRY. That thing.

ORSON. Yes.

KEN. Not now, Orson.

ORSON. It will help me get the money for the movie I want to make of it.

LARRY. Ken just said something marvelous. He said, "May we get back to work?"

ORSON. This tea is lovely.

JOAN. I'll show you the shop.

LARRY. One moment —

JOAN. Darling, Orson ought to have a break —

LARRY. Am I being difficult? I'm being difficult.

JOAN and ORSON. No, no! —

JOAN. No, Orson needs a moment, that's all. He needs to think about what he's going to do about *Chimes at Midnight*. Since this project is proving to be so difficult.

ORSON. Oh, Joan, that's very kind, but —

LARRY. No, it's not!

JOAN. Darling, he is not a hack.

ORSON. Yes, I am! Sometimes I'm a hack!

LARRY. As we both are! So!

ORSON. The only thing is when I'm being a hack I need to take longer breaks.

LARRY. Let me be clear. If I promise to produce *Chimes at Midnight* at the National we can resume this rehearsal —

ORSON. That would be blackmail!

JOAN. Ken says *Chimes at Midnight* is brilliant.

ORSON. Ken is a whore.

KEN. I am a slut, and like all sluts I believe in going back to work.

LARRY. So I'm a slut, then!

ORSON, KEN and JOAN. No, no!

ORSON. All right. So. "Oh, Daisy" —

LARRY. No, no we must clear this up. Orson, you did the thing in Dublin and nobody came.

ORSON. There's a reason for that.

LARRY. What is that?

KEN. Orson —

ORSON. My wife Paola found a chamber pot under our bed and it had not been emptied.

LARRY. Oh, well, of course.

ORSON. And she told the press the Irish clearly liked to wallow in their shit, and, well, that killed the box office.

LARRY. The world is set against you, isn't it.

ORSON. Yes, it is.

KEN. Orson, I do beg you to stop this —

LARRY. I mean, I know your feeling, my dear mother died when I was twelve.

ORSON. My mother died when I was nine.

KEN. And my mother died insane! Let's get back to work!

ORSON. I'm ready.

LARRY. No! Just a moment! You see, I am obliged to tell you you were the inspiration of my youth!

ORSON. No, I wasn't. "Daisy, I never knew" —

LARRY. When I saw *Citizen Kane* —

ORSON. Oh, cut it out!

LARRY. All right, fuck *Citizen Kane*.

ORSON. Thank you.

LARRY. Not at all. So. When I heard your radio show about the Martians landing in New Jersey —

ORSON. Oh, my God, Larry. I was twenty-two!

LARRY. — I was emboldened —

ORSON. I may have even been nineteen!

LARRY. — to direct the film of *Henry the Fifth*.

ORSON. Wait a minute —

LARRY. And from that came all the Shakespeare films I have directed, and with them what little reputation I possess!

ORSON. Wait, I'm responsible for that? For *Henry the Fifth*? And for that *Hamlet* picture?

KEN. Orson, stop.

LARRY. I never give credit for anything, so savor this.

ORSON. You ruined me in Hollywood, and I'm supposed to savor this?

LARRY. And is it possible we are about to learn how I ruined him in Hollywood in 1948?

ORSON. I made my movie of the Scottish play — I slept on the floor!

KEN. Orson —

ORSON. And they said, "This is not how you make a movie out of Shakespeare, no, you must do what Larry does" —

LARRY. Well, I am truly sorry —

ORSON. And I said, "You mean the way he made *Hamlet* look like a bad Joan Crawford movie?"

JOAN. Orson, what are you doing? —

ORSON. *(Overlap.)* "The way he turned *Henry the Fifth* into a scoutmaster?"

LARRY. And the fascinating thing is that you're asking me to put your *Chimes at Midnight* into my theatre!

ORSON. What's wrong with *Chimes at Midnight*?

LARRY. Ken says —

ORSON. Ken says?

KEN. Stop this.

LARRY. He says *Chimes at Midnight* is about loss, betrayal confusion and decay, and I say that is all you have been on about for decades, I'm afraid.

ORSON. Did you say that, Ken?

KEN. I will not be made res-responsible for this catastrophe!

ORSON. Catastrophe? What catastrophe?

LARRY. Oh, stop it, Orson! Back to work!

KEN. Do you know why I tried to bring the two of you together?

ORSON. He doesn't want to know, Ken —

KEN. I — I'd been writing about Broadway for the *New Yorker*, and I was sub—sub-subpoenaed by the House un-Am-m-merican Committee —

JOAN. Good God, Ken, why?

KEN. I don't know. Perhaps it was the stinging review I gave *The Sound of Music*. At any rate, I thought this is m-m-madness, just m-m-madness, I'm down from Oxford only fifteen years and we are living in such frightened times, if I could bring these fearless men together, perhaps it might help! —

LARRY. Darling boy, your arguments are going to have to learn to be a little bit more concise!

KEN. Oh, fuck! All right! He's a great artist! He's a greater fucking artist than you are! *(Silence.)*

ORSON. Oh, Ken.

LARRY. I know that.

ORSON. Oh, Ken, that's not true.

LARRY. Of course it's true. We all know that.

ORSON. Ken, I may have started out as the greater artist but that makes no difference when you're forty-five. I see why you don't want *Chimes at Midnight* at the National, Larry, and I have the solution.

LARRY. You do?

ORSON. I'll play Othello at the National.

LARRY. Othello?

ORSON. I've almost finished my movie of *Othello*. I just need a few more shots, oh, maybe, what, ten thousand dollars.

LARRY. Does it occur to you the National Theatre will not exist simply to finance your films?

ORSON. Larry, I've spent years on that movie, I've shot close-ups in Morocco and reactions to those close-ups two years later in Madrid! —

LARRY. Oh, well, this is a dreadful story. One must go back to Charles Dickens, one must go back to the death of Little Nell, to find a story quite so heartbreaking —

ORSON. Larry —

KEN. I really wish I were dead —

LARRY. And does it occur to you I might like a bash at Othello in my own theatre?

ORSON. Oh, stop it. Othello is a bass, you are a tenor, and sometimes a fucking soprano if you —

LARRY. Orson, I know my limitations. I also know that I can do away with them if I try. You've never directed such a person. You've worked with faithful servants from your radio days, so honored to be directed by you — as they should be — they never give a thought to any possibility but those to which you've led them. Which must be lovely for you, but I'm just not like that, and since we are discussing voice production, you played Othello here ten years ago, and even then you didn't have the breath! And now! Now! —

ORSON. And now I'm fat! I know that! I'm taking diet pills! In fact, I need one now. Sean! *(He grabs pills and water from Sean, swallows. All are paralyzed.)* Can we get back to work? *(As they start back to work.)* Let me just say I am capable of finishing a movie. This picture I just finished — in Hollywood? — is twenty years ahead of its time.

LARRY. In Hollywood, did you say?

ORSON. In Hollywood, yes. Wait 'til they see it at Universal.

KEN. What?

ORSON. It opens with a shot that goes on five minutes, a time bomb ticking in the trunk of a car —

KEN. Wait 'til they see it?

ORSON. Yes, Ken.

KEN. You said they liked it.

ORSON. Well, they liked it when I was shooting it.

KEN. But they haven't seen it?

ORSON. No, of course not —

KEN. Then why have they offered you a five-picture deal?

ORSON. Ken, they haven't offered it yet.

KEN. But —

ORSON. Pay attention!

KEN. You said —

ORSON. It's being edited.

KEN. It's being edited?

ORSON. Yes.

KEN. Then why are you here?

ORSON. What are you talking about?

KEN. Do I understand you've abandoned your first film for Hollywood in twelve years! —

ORSON. I have never abandoned anything in my life!

KEN. *(Overlap.)* On which rest your hopes, your future! — *(Coughing.)*

ORSON. Ken, you're coughing —

KEN. So what!

ORSON. Give me that cigarette!

KEN. No.

LARRY. Just a moment —

ORSON. Ken, it's all right, soon as we're open here I'll go back, I will let them see it! —

KEN. They will see it without you —

ORSON. They have promised me they will not watch it without me!

KEN. They will sneak it!

ORSON. They will not sneak it!

KEN. They will sneak it in Pomona on a Saturday night, and the audience, which will have come to see the main feature, which will be *Francis, the Talking Mule*, will be bewildered and Universal will destroy your film, crying out to everybody who will listen, which will be the rest of Hollywood, "What else could we have done? He was away! He was in Dublin playing in a rewrite of Shakespeare he did when he was at the Todd School for Boys!" And you will be disgraced and you will leave Hollywood for the last time, and you'll be forced to seek your backing for every film you make from now on from a cartel of Bedouins — *(Coughing.)* — who will then seize the print! — *(He is coughing uncontrollably.)*

ORSON. Ken?

JOAN. Shall I call a doctor?

LARRY. *(Going to him.)* Come on, Ken. Put out the cigarette.

KEN. I will not put out the cigarette!

LARRY. Come, come, now, Joan is right, you really ought to be in hospital.

KEN. I only cough in order to conceal my stammer!

ORSON. *(Laughs.)* Ken, come on —

KEN. I'm not sick. I'm just m-m-m-melodramatic! —

SEAN. I have an aunt in Belfast who has emphysema.

JOAN. Sean.

SEAN. I know a test.

ORSON. What test?

SEAN. You light a candle — here — and Ken sees if he can blow it out.

ORSON. Try it.

KEN. I will not.

ORSON. We'll catch it early if you have it. Won't we, Sean.

SEAN. *(Lighting candle.)* Oh, I hope so.

KEN. You will do anything to distract attention from the fact that I know what you should do.

ORSON. Ken, if you take this test Larry and I will start the rehearsal up again.

KEN. Larry?

LARRY. Of course. Of course.

ORSON. Come on, Ken. *(Pause. Ken tries to blow the candle out, several times, and fails. Silence. Finally:)* Well, there, you see? We've caught it early.

JOAN. I'll call a doctor, Ken.

LARRY. I'll do it.

KEN. No, wait. After you have finished the rehearsal.

LARRY. Good Christ, Ken, this is breathing. This is breathing!

ORSON. It's all right, Larry, let's do the rehearsal. Then we can call the doctor.

KEN. Thank you.

ORSON. Ken is a dreadful person, you know.

JOAN. Oh, I'm sure of it.

ORSON. He likes to spank beautiful women. That's why he became a critic.

SEAN. Is it, Ken.

KEN. Well, that's — that's the stated reason.

ORSON. Now, then. Back to work.

LARRY. Off we go. "Oh, Daisy, I never knew I could feel so much," then, darling, you say —

JOAN. *(A modern girl, cheerful, uncaring.)* "Darling, shut the window. They're making such a noise. And the dirt is rising up to here. Everything will get filthy."

LARRY. All right. And then I say — I say —

ORSON. That was good, Joan.

JOAN. Is that what you want, then.

LARRY. Darling, you're marvelous. You're really marvelous, well, it's her wit, it's delicious. But there's a serpent in that garden, darling. It can keep us from loving the people that we play. That is my secret, and I give it to you, Joan, and I never pass along my secrets, never. But there it is. You must love her. I'm sorry, old cock.

ORSON. But Daisy is a fool.

LARRY. Then how am I to play my fellow, who must love her?

ORSON. Your fellow is a helpless and pathetic idiot.

LARRY. Then how can I love him, Orson?

ORSON. You can't love a helpless and pathetic idiot?

LARRY. Darling —

JOAN. That's an interesting question he just asked you.

LARRY. Darling — help.

JOAN. All right. *(Sweetly, with love; she does try.)* "Darling, shut the window. They're making such a noise. And the dirt is rising up to here. Everything will get filthy."

LARRY. Well, now, that's it, isn't it. Now I feel I can proceed. You do see what I mean, Orson — *(Orson throws a chair across the room.)*

ORSON. I'm sorry, Ken.

KEN. Please.

LARRY. Well, dear boy, if it's that important to you —

ORSON. It's not important to me. It doesn't matter to me how either of you say anything because there's going to be a lot of sound.

LARRY. Sound?

ORSON. Well, there's a herd of rhinoceroses in the street and I just thought somehow that —

LARRY. Surely that can be suggested without wiping out our voices! —

ORSON. This is a play about Fascism, Larry. Fascism is noisy. But go ahead. Play the scene the way you want to. Of course I don't understand why she leaves you in five minutes if she's so goddamned sweet and loving, but go ahead. Play it like that movie you made with Vivien, play it like Lord Nelson and Lady Hamilton, go ahead. Winston Churchill loved that movie, well, of course he did, very beautiful, so romantic, it helped to get you through the war. And if you want to turn this play into something that will help England through the war, that's fine, you do it wonderfully, the only problem is the war is over! And Joanie's young, Joanie's not interested in the war, Joanie's interested in the future, which is what I thought this show was all about, the future, but perhaps I'm wrong —

LARRY. Are you suggesting I'm not interested in the future?

ORSON. I'm suggesting that you chose this part that cries out, "I'm a little man," a clerk, whose life is going nowhere and who spends his time pining for a girl who is self-evidently a little twit! You picked the part, you picked the play, I didn't, I hate this play! —

LARRY. You hate this —

ORSON. Don't get superior, Larry. Don't get ethical! You obviously don't think much of it either, or you wouldn't be maneuvering your brilliant, tough-minded fiancée into trying to love this girl. No, you don't like it, I don't like it, but we're smart men, Larry, we can make it work. And if we're going to do that we have to reach a decision about who's directing it, and I think — Sean, give me the script, let me just look — it says here I am the director! All right. All right, then. What shall I say? Oh, yes. I think your character's an idiot. I think your character's a loser. And if you have to love him love him, or can you only fall in love with kings who break the hearts of their best friends and narcissistic vaudevillians who imitate American blues singers when they hear their sons have died? I'm sure that's not true, I'm completely sure, because you're an actor, a great actor, and an actor loves everybody, isn't that right? Even characters who disappear! And, Larry, this man disappears. And let me tell you something else. We've got to create some suspense in this production, I mean, there's no suspense whatsoever in this stupid play because it's clear from the beginning that everyone in town is going to turn into a rhino and only our brave little loser here is going to stand alone. And if you can tell me how to build suspense with that, if you can tell me how to keep an audience emotionally and intellectually interested in that, I promise you, Larry, I'll go down on you. So where is the suspense? How do we keep them in suspense? I'll tell you. We keep them wondering all evening if Larry Olivier is going to have the guts to disappear. Larry Olivier, who has been fucking audiences for twenty years now with his new-found confidence from World War Two, is he really going to play this man who no one notices. This is what people are like now, Larry, these are the dreary lives they're leading now, this is what the audience is looking for these days, and this is what everybody's wondering, is Larry Olivier finally ready to disappear and join the modern age? Show us that you can, Larry, I promise you, there won't be a dry seat in the house! Joan, say that line, and say it like I told you!

JOAN. (*The modern girl.*) "Shut the window, darling, they're making such a noise. And the dust is rising even up to here. Everything will get filthy."

LARRY. And I'm supposed to love that?

ORSON and JOAN. YES! *(Pause.)*

LARRY. And so I shut the window. And I say, "I'm not afraid of anything as long as we're together. My love, my dear love, let me kiss you." And I kiss her. *(He does.)* Yes! And I say, "I never dreamed I could feel so much emotion," but I'll have to say it loud because there will be all that noise. Good. Good, Orson. You Americans have always been so marvelous at overlapping! But then what do I do? I know. I'll do everything. The dusting, the table, the chair, the pot of tea — and go ahead, dear boy, set it in England, that should upset them altogether, splendid — I'll do all this and I'll become a blur, and that will drive the poor girl out into the hooves of my rival, yes, that's the reason that I stand alone, because I am a blur, I am alone because no one can see me! Well, dear God, this will be the new Olivier.

KEN. Bravo! Yes! Yes!

ORSON. So, you see. *(He begins to dance, a soft-shoe; He hums.)*

JOAN. Orson, what are you singing?

ORSON. *(Dancing.)* A song I wrote when I was at the Todd School for Boys.

LARRY. *(Very happy.)* Dear boy, you know you are absurd. You know this.

ORSON. *(Dancing.)* Yes, I do.

LARRY. I remember a dance I did in *The Entertainer*. Might I? —

ORSON, KEN and JOAN. Yes! *(And Orson and Larry dance together, a soft-shoe, when suddenly Sean, who has momentarily left, reenters in a hurry.)*

SEAN. Larry, your wife is here. She wants to see you.

LARRY. Where is she?

SEAN. In the car.

LARRY. What is she doing?

SEAN. Sitting.

LARRY. I suppose I should go and greet her.

SEAN. Was she Scarlett O'Hara?

LARRY. *(To Orson.)* I know you adore her, old boy. I can see why she means so much to you, and I have to say, I would adore her, too, if I were you. But I'm not you, and I don't adore her, I love her, and she loves oblivion, and I cannot stand it. This lust for oblivion she has, which is not her fault, she's ill, it terrifies me. What would you do if you were in love with someone with the plague? What would you do? Would you allow yourself to catch it? *(Pause. He leaves, No one speaks. Vivien enters.)*

VIVIEN. Hello. It seemed you were all on break, so I —

ORSON. How wonderful to see you, Vivien.

VIVIEN. I have something for you, darling, but I don't want to interrupt. I know how it is when people just barge into a rehearsal.

ORSON. Vivien? This is Joan Plowright and Kenneth Tynan.

VIVIEN. Miss Plowright.

JOAN. Miss Leigh.

VIVIEN. I saw you on this very stage. Larry and I saw you. In *Roots*. You gave such a beautiful performance.

JOAN. Thank you.

VIVIEN. Larry and I came round.

JOAN. Yes.

VIVIEN. I remember at the end — what was it you said at the end — you'd been in this dreadful situation, this awful poverty, and you said — you said —

JOAN. I said, "I'm be — I'm beg — "

VIVIEN. Mr. Tynan I remember, wrote so well about it. Do you remember, Mr. Tynan?

KEN. Oh, no — n-n —

VIVIEN. You wrote you stepped out into the August night, shattered —

KEN. July —

VIVIEN. I'm sorry?

KEN. July night. It's not im —

VIVIEN. July night. I'm sorry

KEN. That's all right.

VIVIEN. Thank you. And you said it was what Miss Plowright said right at the end that moved you, as it moved me certainly —

JOAN. Oh, I —

VIVIEN. No. Yes. When you said, "I'm beginning. I'm beginning!" It was so very fine.

JOAN. You are more than kind.

VIVIEN. Well, I never got to tell you that night, you know what with all the —

JOAN. Dear, yes, that night with all the —

VIVIEN. Fuss. Mr. Tynan?

KEN. K-k-k-Ken — *(Coughs very badly.)*

VIVIEN. You're ill, aren't you, Ken.

KEN. Well, it's nothing really that I —

VIVIEN. They've probably told you dire things about it. They've told me the same things, well, you know, lungs, in my case it's TB. I'm only saying they're trying to scare us, and for Christ's sake don't

64

let Larry talk to you about your breathing, I mean, what does he know really about breathing? He can breathe! My point is we both have time, plenty of time to clean up whatever mess we've made, which is all one can really ask, I think —

KEN. I would have to be Methuselah to —

VIVIEN. No, you wouldn't, Ken. No more than any of us.

JOAN. I admired you so much in *A Streetcar Named Desire*.

VIVIEN. Thank you. Larry directed me in it on the stage here, but do you mean the film?

JOAN. I mean the film.

VIVIEN. Yes, that was better, actually. Kazan made me change everything I'd done for Larry.

JOAN. I know.

VIVIEN. Is Larry still brooding about that, do you think?

JOAN. I don't know. *(Pause.)* I'm sorry. Would you like me to find Larry?

VIVIEN. If you can do that, you're a better man than I am, Gunga Din. I'm sorry. Yes, I would. That's very kind of you.

JOAN. I won't be a minute.

VIVIEN. Oh, no, no. Be a minute. No more than five minutes, though, I beg you, or I shall go mad, which is not a figure of speech with me, I'm afraid.

JOAN. Five minutes, then. *(She goes.)*

VIVIEN. Ken?

KEN. Yes?

VIVIEN. Do you have a cigarette?

KEN. I — do you really think that's —

VIVIEN. Please. *(He gets out cigarettes, hands her one.)* Thank you.

KEN. You know, I've always meant to — do you recall a review about your Cleopatra —

VIVIEN. You may light it, sir.

KEN. Of course, of course, I — *(Lights it.)*

VIVIEN. Thank you. *(Inhales.)* Oh, that's good. You have one, too.

KEN. I —

ORSON. Vivien —

VIVIEN. Orson? *(Orson is silent.)*

KEN. Here —

VIVIEN. No, no, Ken, don't light it, let me — *(She lights Ken cigarette with her own. He takes it and inhales.)* Isn't that good?

KEN. Yes. *(They smoke in silence for a moment.)*

VIVIEN. That's enough, I guess. *(She puts out her cigarette and takes his. She puts that out, too.)* Could you find Larry, Ken? It feels like half an hour.

KEN. Of course. *(He hurries out.)*

ORSON. Are you all right?

VIVIEN. I'm a little manic, I'm afraid. Larry's leaving me. Let me show you what I've got for you. What is the name of that darling boy, Sean! Sean!

SEAN. Yes, Vivien.

VIVIEN. It's Miss Leigh, if you don't mind. Sean, would you get the? — *(Sean hurries out.)* It's your fault Larry's leaving me.

ORSON. My fault?

VIVIEN. It's when you did that marvelous radio programme about the Martians landing in New Jersey —

ORSON. Oh, that was many years —

VIVIEN. Shut up. Who gives a shit that it was years ago. Stop that. People fled their homes, Orson, people killed themselves, because you made them believe in all your Martians. And Larry was so jealous, and then I got the role of Scarlett O'Hara in *Gone with the Wind* and he was devastated. And he took it out on your show about the Martians, and I said, "Larry, oh my darling boy, you have moved people," and he turned on me and he said, "No one has taken to the roads. No one has actually committed suicide." Larry sets very high standards for himself. *(As Sean enters with a teacart, on which is a steak dinner under a cover on a silver platter, and a bottle of red wine, opened:)* Here we are!

ORSON. Oh, Vivien —

VIVIEN. Now, don't say a word, Sean, tie this napkin around his neck, you know how he gets. I remember hearing how you used to eat these steaks when you were young and everybody loved you, and I find that when one works with Larry one needs to be reminded of when one was loved —

ORSON. I'm very, very touched —

VIVIEN. I wish Larry would come. I'm getting to that point in the mania where I become unpleasant, and I don't want that to happen 'til I'm on the plane, where I can assault a stewardess or something —

ORSON. The plane?

VIVIEN. I've got to be at Heathrow in an hour —

ORSON. You just got here!

VIVIEN. I have a performance in New York tomorrow night!

ORSON. This is insane!

VIVIEN.   Could you put that just a little bit more delicately? Although you're right, oh, the depression that comes after this one, the electric shock they're going to have to give me in New York is going to turn the lights off all over the West Side, it'll be the most terrifying thing since your Martians landed in New Jersey, well, how is it, is it any good?

ORSON.   It is so good.

VIVIEN.   Good. What's this I hear about your playing a fat old man in Dublin to empty houses, you sexy thing, you.

ORSON.   Falstaff —

VIVIEN.   Of course! Falstaff! And I have never seen it. I must see it! You must come to Notley and give us a command performance- *(She stops; Orson pours her a glass of wine; she takes it.)* Why did they have to give me Scarlett?

ORSON.   Because you were born to play it.

VIVIEN.   Oh, fuck off.

ORSON.   I have a confession for you, Vivien.

VIVIEN.   Oh, boy.

ORSON.   You remember how much in demand I was then?

VIVIEN.   Oh, yes. Yes. It was so exciting—

ORSON.   Vivien, they offered me the role of Scarlett O'Hara.

VIVIEN.   They did?

ORSON.   Now, don't laugh! I was thinner then!

VIVIEN.   Well, why didn't you take it, you bastard? I wouldn't be here in this awful place! —

ORSON.   Because I saw your screen test and I said, "She's the survivor. She's the role. I withdraw my name at once from your consideration."

VIVIEN.   The survivor.

ORSON.   You know why he can't get the money for his movie of the Scottish play?

VIVIEN.   I'm not sure I want to hear —

ORSON.   Because who wants to see, close up, the face of a man who gets rid of people because they remind him of loss and confusion, which are written on your lovely face so much that you will always be a great star. Don't wait for him. Just leave, right now, and let him live without the one thing that will teach him what he needs to know.

VIVIEN.   Don't ever speak of him that way again. To me or anyone.

ORSON.   I'm sorry.

VIVIEN.   And what are you doing still playing Falstaff?

ORSON. I'm going to make a movie of it!

VIVIEN. Oh, bless you! And you worked on it in my garden!

ORSON. I owe it all to you, and your garden, and you're the first person I'm going to tell, I have a plan to get the money, I have this Hungarian investor —

VIVIEN. But I thought you didn't need those people anymore, Sean told me you're back in Hollywood! —

ORSON. They wouldn't let me drive onto the lot at Universal.

VIVIEN. What?

ORSON. They wouldn't let me drive onto the lot. I'm sorry, Sean. They said, "You've had your chance," they hate the picture, and I'm finished there. And that is it, so —

VIVIEN. Oh, my poor Orson.

ORSON. Don't call me that.

VIVIEN. I'm sorry.

ORSON. Well, there's no reason to be sad! I have a plan with this Hungarian, I can make *Chimes at Midnight* and no one will even know I'm making it.

VIVIEN. Sean, run, get the other bottle, open it, let it breathe, if you'll pardon the expression!

ORSON. *(As Sean leaves.)* My God, you know what? There's a part for you in this plan!

VIVIEN. You want to restore my film career? *(Calls.)* Sean!

ORSON. I am going to restore your film career! I am going to restore mine!

VIVIEN. *(Overlap.)* Restoring my film career is impossible. There's only one thing that can help me, Orson.

ORSON. What?

VIVIEN. I must fuck Sean.

ORSON. Well, fine, but I want to tell you my plan.

SEAN. *(Reentering with wine.)* Here you are, Vivien! —

VIVIEN. Thank you. Now, come on, honey, dance with me.

ORSON. Listen to me.

VIVIEN. *(Dancing with Sean.)* Oh, God, why didn't I bring my record player? Do you have a record player?

SEAN. No,

ORSON. Will you listen to me, please?

VIVIEN *(Overlap.)* I don't care! I didn't bring the record!

ORSON. WILL YOU STOP DANCING AND LISTEN TO MY PLAN? AND SHUT UP! *(Vivien and Sean stop dancing.)*

VIVIEN. Orson? Are you all right? *(Orson says nothing.)* Do you know something? We can stop right now. Because if we keep up what we're doing right now I shall become excited and really rather terrifying and Larry will come in and it will frighten him. And when he's frightened people get hurt. Poor Larry. But people get hurt.

ORSON. Oh, Vivien.

VIVIEN. What is it? What's the matter, darling?

ORSON. Do you know what I heard while I was in the States?

VIVIEN. What?

ORSON. The Todd School for Boys is closed. It's closed. For good.

VIVIEN. Oh, Christ. I'm getting anxious. Are you getting anxious?

ORSON. No, I am not getting anxious! Here's my plan. The Hungarian doesn't want to make *Chimes at Midnight*, he wants me to make another picture.

VIVIEN *(Disoriented.)* Another picture.

ORSON. Not *Chimes at Midnight*. But on the plane I thought, I could shoot *Chimes at Midnight* at the same time, same sets, same actors, and just not tell the Hungarian.

VIVIEN. Orson, the Hungarian will know.

ORSON. *Chimes at Midnight* will echo down the corridors of time.

VIVIEN. Sean, let's dance.

ORSON. Vivien, please. Please.

VIVIEN. *(Dancing with Sean.)* I can't do this without the record. Why didn't I bring the record, why?

ORSON. Vivien, what's the matter?

SEAN. I could hum it.

VIVIEN. Yes, oh, that's adorable! Can you hum the waltz from *Gone with the Wind*?

SEAN. No.

VIVIEN. All right, you hum it, Orson.

ORSON. I am not going to sit here and hum the waltz from *Gone with the Wind*.

VIVIEN. You have a beautiful voice!

ORSON. *(Overlap.)* You want to dance while I hum the waltz from *Gone with the Wind*, and then we talk about tracking shots in *Citizen Kane*?

VIVIEN. *(Pulling Sean to her.)* Sean, what's the matter, for Christ's sake?

ORSON. I want to talk about the future!

VIVIEN. We are not going to talk about the future!

ORSON. Is that asking too much? LET ME AT LEAST TALK ABOUT IT!

SEAN. *(Pulling away.)* Stop this, will you? What if Larry comes in?

VIVIEN. That is the point, you stupid Mick!

SEAN. Listen, you bitch!

ORSON. Vivien, get hold of yourself!

VIVIEN. My God, you're fat! You're fat! And look at how much I was feeding you!

SEAN. *(She's going for the cart.)* Vivien, what are you —

VIVIEN. Give it to me! It's going to kill him! *(She wrenches the cart free of Sean, hurling things off of it.)* Larry! LARRY! LARRY! *(Larry runs on.)*

LARRY. Vivien —

VIVIEN. Oh, my Larry! *(She breaks down in his arms. Orson watches speechless. Joan and Ken come on. Joan watches, helpless, and then quietly goes back out.)*

LARRY. I'll take you to Notley. Sean? —

VIVIEN. I won't go to Notley.

LARRY. Darling, I'll call ahead, they'll put out a light supper for us —

VIVIEN. Larry, you're going to have to sell Notley.

LARRY. I won't sell it.

VIVIEN. You think Joan is going to want to live at Notley? *(Larry is silent; they admit that it is over.)* I need to get to the airport.

LARRY. That's out of the question —

VIVIEN. Let me go, please.

LARRY. I'll come with you.

VIVIEN. I don't want you to come with me. It would be horrible if you came with me.

LARRY. Well, you're not going alone.

VIVIEN. I'll be fine. Last week I had a treatment and I went on stage two hours later and played beautifully, thank you very much.

LARRY. I won't have it. I won't send you there alone.

VIVIEN. I want Ken.

LARRY. Ken?

VIVIEN. Yes. *(Pause.)*

LARRY. Ken?

KEN. But I must — finish this — *(He gestures to the audience; he must finish his narrating duties.)*

VIVIEN. Come on, Ken. *(He goes to her. She starts out with him ... She stops and says:)* Macbeth. *(Silence.)* Macbeth. Macbeth. Macbeth. Macbeth. Macbeth. *(More silence. She leaves with Ken.)*

LARRY. Sean?

SEAN. Yes, Larry.

LARRY. Get out.

SEAN. OK. *(He starts out, stops.)* Orson?

ORSON. *(Waves him off wordlessly; Sean goes.)*

LARRY. I think — I think we must get to work, old boy.

ORSON. Work?

LARRY. I think I must. Otherwise …

ORSON. Of course.

LARRY. So Daisy's left him, she's gone off to become a rhino with the man she loves, my fellow is alone. He's looking in the mirror, right, I guess he wants to see if he's to be a rhino, if there are tell-tale rhino signs on him —

ORSON. A horn or something —

LARRY. Well, you know, or scales — *(Both laugh nervously.)*

ORSON. I'm sorry, Larry. I upset her, and I know how her illness affects you and I understand now, and please —

LARRY. So. Where shall we place the mirror?

ORSON. I don't know. Right here. Just — here. OK?

LARRY. Yes. *(He looks out toward the audience, at an imaginary mirror.)*

ORSON. Larry? *(Silence.)* Larry?

LARRY. I'm afraid I'm going to have to let you go, old man.

ORSON. Oh, Larry.

LARRY. Don't plead, Orson. It frightens me to hear you plead. Don't plead. Ever again. *(Orson is silent. Silence between them. Joan enters.)*

JOAN. *(Addresses us.)* I'm the only person in this play who's still alive. So if you'll just let me wrap this up. *Rhinoceros* opened on the 28th of April, 1960. There was praise, there was blame, we moved on. Larry and I were married. There are three marvelous children. We had ten fine years at the National, with Ken, many successes, really rebirth after rebirth for Larry, some of his best years. He played Othello, he deepened his voice and played Othello, and he was the animal that Ken had always known he was, that I knew he was. Then Ken persuaded him to put on a new play that was critical of Winston Churchill in the war, and Larry knew no fear by now, he said, "Fuck it, let's do it," but the Board stopped it and soon afterward they edged him out, and Ken, and it was over. Then Larry contracted a wasting muscular disease and never acted on the stage again. He managed to do films somehow, to put something in the larder for the children. I don't know how he did it. Sometimes I'd come upon him weeping, once he was watching

71

telly and there was *That Hamilton Woman* playing, with him and Vivien, and he was weeping and saying, "That was love, now. That was real love." I don't think he saw me.

LARRY. Darling?

JOAN. Yes?

LARRY. What happened to Vivien?

JOAN. She died of TB, at the age of fifty-three.

ORSON. What happened to Ken?

JOAN. He died of emphysema, at the age of fifty-three.

ORSON. And Sean?

JOAN. I don't know.

ORSON. What happened to me, Joan?

JOAN. Well, you — you —

ORSON. Come on, Joan. You're a straight shooter.

JOAN. You never worked in the theatre again.

ORSON. And movies? Did I? —

JOAN. You managed to start one new movie and complete it.

ORSON. Just one?

JOAN. Yes.

ORSON. How long did I live?

JOAN. Twenty-five more years. *(Pause.)*

ORSON. What was the movie?

JOAN. *Chimes at Midnight.*

ORSON. Was it any good?

JOAN. Well, your investors didn't give you enough money to have decent sound, and so the sound is dreadful, and it's Shakespeare, so —

ORSON. I see.

JOAN. But Orson? It's beautiful.

ORSON. How is it at the end when I go to my best friend's coronation and he pretends he doesn't know me?

JOAN. Shattering.

ORSON. No other movies? At all?

JOAN. There was a documentary.

ORSON. A documentary?

JOAN. It was unusual, it was remarkable actually —

ORSON. Was it ahead of its time?

JOAN. Yes.

ORSON. Shit.

JOAN. And some television. Serious television, Orson —

ORSON. Oh, my God —

JOAN. And the picture you'd done for Universal —

ORSON. *Touch of Evil.* They butchered it. It's my fault, Ken was right —

JOAN. It's shown now in the version you wanted all along.

ORSON. Did — did any of these movies manage to eclipse peoples' memory of *Citizen Kane*?

JOAN. No.

ORSON. What a strange life. *(Pause.)* You know who got me *Touch of Evil*? Charlton Heston. They wanted him for the hero, he was a big star then, he'd just done Moses in *The Ten Commandments*, and I'd signed just to play the villain, I thought I'd pick up a little cash and shoot a few more minutes of *Othello*, and they called Heston and they said, "We've got Welles," and he thought they meant they had me to direct, and he said, "Welles? You've got Welles? I'll do it." Isn't that wonderful? It was because of *Citizen Kane*, but, still, it's wonderful. The world was not set against me after all. Moses led me out the wilderness and back to Hollywood.

LARRY. Dear boy —

ORSON. I'm sorry.

LARRY. We have run out of time for stories.

ORSON. Have we?

LARRY. Oh, yes. We have heard the chimes at midnight. That we have. *(Pause.)*

JOAN. *(To us.)* Good night.

End of Play

PROPERTY LIST

Robe, brandy, hot water (SEAN)
Food, tableware (SEAN)
Phones (VIVIEN, LARRY)
Scones, jam (JOAN)
Cigarettes (KEN, SEAN)
Script (SEAN)
Tea service (SEAN)
Sugar (JOAN)
Pills, water (SEAN)
Candle, lighter or matches (SEAN)
Chair (ORSON)
Teacart, steak dinner, bottle of red wine, glasses, napkins (SEAN)
Wine (ORSON, SEAN)

SOUND EFFECTS

Phone ring

NEW PLAYS

★ **THE EXONERATED by Jessica Blank and Erik Jensen.** Six interwoven stories paint a picture of an American criminal justice system gone horribly wrong and six brave souls who persevered to survive it. "The #1 play of the year...intense and deeply affecting..." *–NY Times*. "Riveting. Simple, honest storytelling that demands reflection." *–A.P.* "Artful and moving...pays tribute to the resilience of human hearts and minds." *–Variety*. "Stark...riveting...cunningly orchestrated." *–The New Yorker*. "Hard-hitting, powerful, and socially relevant." *–Hollywood Reporter*. [7M, 3W] ISBN: 0-8222-1946-8

★ **STRING FEVER by Jacquelyn Reingold.** Lily juggles the big issues: turning forty, artificial insemination and the elusive scientific Theory of Everything in this Off-Broadway comedy hit. "Applies the elusive rules of string theory to the conundrums of one woman's love life. Think *Sex and the City* meets *Copenhagen*." *–NY Times*. "A funny offbeat and touching look at relationships...an appealing romantic comedy populated by oddball characters." *–NY Daily News*. "Where kooky, zany, and madcap meet...whimsically winsome." *–NY Magazine*. "STRING FEVER will have audience members happily stringing along." *–TheaterMania.com*. "Reingold's language is surprising, inventive, and unique." *–nytheatre.com*. "...[a] whimsical comic voice." *–Time Out*. [3M, 3W (doubling)] ISBN: 0-8222-1952-2

★ **DEBBIE DOES DALLAS adapted by Erica Schmidt, composed by Andrew Sherman, conceived by Susan L. Schwartz.** A modern morality tale told as a comic musical of tragic proportions as the classic film is brought to the stage. "A scream! A saucy, tongue-in-cheek romp." *–The New Yorker*. "Hilarious! DEBBIE manages to have it all: beauty, brains and a great sense of humor!" *–Time Out*. "Shamelessly silly, shrewdly self-aware and proud of being naughty. Great fun!" *–NY Times*. "Racy and raucous, a lighthearted, fast-paced thoroughly engaging and hilarious send-up." *–NY Daily News*. [3M, 5W] ISBN: 0-8222-1955-7

★ **THE MYSTERY PLAYS by Roberto Aguirre-Sacasa.** Two interrelated one acts, loosely based on the tradition of the medieval mystery plays. "... stylish, spine-tingling...Mr. Aguirre-Sacasa uses standard tricks of horror stories, borrowing liberally from masters like Kafka, Lovecraft, Hitchcock...But his mastery of the genre is his own...irresistible." *–NY Times*. "Undaunted by the special-effects limitations of theatre, playwright and *Marvel* comic-book writer Roberto Aguirre-Sacasa maps out some creepy twilight zones in THE MYSTERY PLAYS, an engaging, related pair of one acts...The theatre may rarely deliver shocks equivalent to, say, *Dawn of the Dead*, but Aguirre-Sacasa's work is fine compensation." *–Time Out*. [4M, 2W] ISBN: 0-8222-2038-5

★ **THE JOURNALS OF MIHAIL SEBASTIAN by David Auburn.** This epic one-man play spans eight tumultuous years and opens a uniquely personal window on the Romanian Holocaust and the Second World War. "Powerful." *–NY Times*. "[THE JOURNALS OF MIHAIL SEBASTIAN] allows us to glimpse the idiosyncratic effects of that awful history on one intelligent, pragmatic, recognizably real man..." *–NY Newsday*. [3M, 5W] ISBN: 0-8222-2006-7

★ **LIVING OUT by Lisa Loomer.** The story of the complicated relationship between a Salvadoran nanny and the Anglo lawyer she works for. "A stellar new play. Searingly funny." *–The New Yorker*. "Both generous and merciless, equally enjoyable and disturbing." *–NY Newsday*. "A bitingly funny new comedy. The plight of working mothers is explored from two pointedly contrasting perspectives in this sympathetic, sensitive new play." *–Variety*. [2M, 6W] ISBN: 0-8222-1994-8

DRAMATISTS PLAY SERVICE, INC.
440 Park Avenue South, New York, NY 10016 212-683-8960 Fax 212-213-1539
postmaster@dramatists.com www.dramatists.com

NEW PLAYS

★ **MATCH by Stephen Belber.** Mike and Lisa Davis interview a dancer and choreographer about his life, but it is soon evident that their agenda will either ruin or inspire them—and definitely change their lives forever. "Prolific laughs and ear-to-ear smiles." –*NY Magazine.* "Uproariously funny, deeply moving, enthralling theater. Stephen Belber's MATCH has great beauty and tenderness, and abounds in wit." –*NY Daily News.* "Three and a half out of four stars." –*USA Today.* "A theatrical steeplechase that leads straight from outrageous bitchery to unadorned, heartfelt emotion." –*Wall Street Journal.* [2M, 1W] ISBN: 0-8222-2020-2

★ **HANK WILLIAMS: LOST HIGHWAY by Randal Myler and Mark Harelik.** The story of the beloved and volatile country-music legend Hank Williams, featuring twenty-five of his most unforgettable songs. "[LOST HIGHWAY has] the exhilarating feeling of Williams on stage in a particular place on a particular night...serves up classic country with the edges raw and the energy hot...By the end of the play, you've traveled on a profound emotional journey: LOST HIGHWAY transports its audience and communicates the inspiring message of the beauty and richness of Williams' songs...forceful, clear-eyed, moving, impressive." –*Rolling Stone.* "...honors a very particular musical talent with care and energy... smart, sweet, poignant." –*NY Times.* [7M, 3W] ISBN: 0-8222-1985-9

★ **THE STORY by Tracey Scott Wilson.** An ambitious black newspaper reporter goes against her editor to investigate a murder and finds the *best* story...but at what cost? "A singular new voice...deeply emotional, deeply intellectual, and deeply musical..." –*The New Yorker.* "...a conscientious and absorbing new drama..." –*NY Times.* "...a riveting, tough-minded drama about race, reporting and the truth..." –*A.P.* "... a stylish, attention-holding script that ends on a chilling note that will leave viewers with much to talk about." –*Curtain Up.* [2M, 7W (doubling, flexible casting)] ISBN: 0-8222-1998-0

★ **OUR LADY OF 121st STREET by Stephen Adly Guirgis.** The body of Sister Rose, beloved Harlem nun, has been stolen, reuniting a group of life-challenged childhood friends who square off as they wait for her return. "A scorching and dark new comedy... Mr. Guirgis has one of the finest imaginations for dialogue to come along in years." –*NY Times.* "Stephen Guirgis may be the best playwright in America under forty." –*NY Magazine.* [8M, 4W] ISBN: 0-8222-1965-4

★ **HOLLYWOOD ARMS by Carrie Hamilton and Carol Burnett.** The coming-of-age story of a dreamer who manages to escape her bleak life and follow her romantic ambitions to stardom. Based on Carol Burnett's bestselling autobiography, *One More Time.* "...pure theatre and pure entertainment..." –*Talkin' Broadway.* "...a warm, fuzzy evening of theatre." –*BrodwayBeat.com.* "...chuckles and smiles of recognition or surprise flow naturally...a remarkable slice of life." –*TheatreScene.net.* [5M, 5W, 1 girl] ISBN: 0-8222-1959-X

★ **INVENTING VAN GOGH by Steven Dietz.** A haunting and hallucinatory drama about the making of art, the obsession to create and the fine line that separates truth from myth. "Like a van Gogh painting, Dietz's story is a gorgeous example of excess—one that remakes reality with broad, well-chosen brush strokes. At evening's end, we're left with the author's resounding opinions on art and artifice, and provoked by his constant query into which is greater: van Gogh's art or his violent myth." –*Phoenix New Times.* "Dietz's writing is never simple. It is always brilliant. Shaded, compressed, direct, lucid—he frames his subject with a remarkable understanding of painting as a physical experience." –*Tucson Citizen.* [4M, 1W] ISBN: 0-8222-1954-9

DRAMATISTS PLAY SERVICE, INC.
440 Park Avenue South, New York, NY 10016 212-683-8960 Fax 212-213-1539
postmaster@dramatists.com www.dramatists.com

NEW PLAYS

★ **INTIMATE APPAREL by Lynn Nottage.** The moving and lyrical story of a turn-of-the-century black seamstress whose gifted hands and sewing machine are the tools she uses to fashion her dreams from the whole cloth of her life's experiences. "…Nottage's play has a delicacy and eloquence that seem absolutely right for the time she is depicting…" *–NY Daily News.* "…thoughtful, affecting…The play offers poignant commentary on an era when the cut and color of one's dress—and of course, skin—determined whom one could and could not marry, sleep with, even talk to in public." *–Variety.* [2M, 4W] ISBN: 0-8222-2009-1

★ **BROOKLYN BOY by Donald Margulies.** A witty and insightful look at what happens to a writer when his novel hits the bestseller list. "The characters are beautifully drawn, the dialogue sparkles…" *–nytheatre.com.* "Few playwrights have the mastery to smartly investigate so much through a laugh-out-loud comedy that combines the vintage subject matter of successful writer-returning-to-ethnic-roots with the familiar mid-life crisis." *–Show Business Weekly.* [4M, 3W] ISBN: 0-8222-2074-1

★ **CROWNS by Regina Taylor.** Hats become a springboard for an exploration of black history and identity in this celebratory musical play. "Taylor pulls off a Hat Trick: She scores thrice, turning CROWNS into an artful amalgamation of oral history, fashion show, and musical theater…" *–TheatreMania.com.* "…wholly theatrical…Ms. Taylor has created a show that seems to arise out of spontaneous combustion, as if a bevy of department-store customers simultaneously decided to stage a revival meeting in the changing room." *–NY Times.* [1M, 6W (2 musicians)] ISBN: 0-8222-1963-8

★ **EXITS AND ENTRANCES by Athol Fugard.** The story of a relationship between a young playwright on the threshold of his career and an aging actor who has reached the end of his. "[Fugard] can say more with a single line than most playwrights convey in an entire script…Paraphrasing the title, it's safe to say this drama, making its memorable entrance into our consciousness, is unlikely to exit as long as a theater exists for exceptional work." *–Variety.* "A thought-provoking, elegant and engrossing new play…" *–Hollywood Reporter.* [2M] ISBN: 0-8222-2041-5

★ **BUG by Tracy Letts.** A thriller featuring a pair of star-crossed lovers in an Oklahoma City motel facing a bug invasion, paranoia, conspiracy theories and twisted psychological motives. "…obscenely exciting…top-flight craftsmanship. Buckle up and brace yourself…" *–NY Times.* "…[a] thoroughly outrageous and thoroughly entertaining play…the possibility of enemies, real and imagined, to squash has never been more theatrical." *–A.P.* [3M, 2W] ISBN: 0-8222-2016-4

★ **THOM PAIN (BASED ON NOTHING) by Will Eno.** An ordinary man muses on childhood, yearning, disappointment and loss, as he draws the audience into his last-ditch plea for empathy and enlightenment. "It's one of those treasured nights in the theater—treasured nights anywhere, for that matter—that can leave you both breathless with exhilaration and…in a puddle of tears." *–NY Times.* "Eno's words…are familiar, but proffered in a way that is constantly contradictory to our expectations. Beckett is certainly among his literary ancestors." *–nytheatre.com.* [1M] ISBN: 0-8222-2076-8

★ **THE LONG CHRISTMAS RIDE HOME by Paula Vogel.** Past, present and future collide on a snowy Christmas Eve for a troubled family of five. "…[a] lovely and hauntingly original family drama…a work that breathes so much life into the theater." *–Time Out.* "…[a] delicate visual feast…" *–NY Times.* "…brutal and lovely…the overall effect is magical." *–NY Newsday.* [3M, 3W] ISBN: 0-8222-2003-2

DRAMATISTS PLAY SERVICE, INC.
440 Park Avenue South, New York, NY 10016 212-683-8960 Fax 212-213-1539
postmaster@dramatists.com www.dramatists.com